Spanish

Online Diagnostic Test

Go to **Schaums.com** to launch the Schaum's Diagnostic Test.

This convenient application provides a 30-question test that will pinpoint areas of strength and weakness to help you focus your study. Questions cover all aspects of Spanish grammar covered by this book. With a question-bank that rotates daily, the Schaum's Online Test also allows you to check your progress and readiness for final exams.

Other titles featured in Schaum's Online Diagnostic Test:

Spanish

—————— Second Edition

Conrad J. Schmitt

Abridgement Editors:
Joseph R. Jones
and Margaret E. W. Jones

New York   Chicago   San Francisco   Lisbon   London   Madrid   Mexico City
Milan   New Delhi   San Juan   Seoul   Singapore   Sydney   Toronto

The *McGraw·Hill* Companies

1 2 3 4 5 6 7 8 9 10 11 12 13 14 15   DOC/DOC   1 9 8 7 6 5 4 3 2 1

ISBN 978-0-07-176056-0
MHID   0-07-176056-3

Library of Congress Cataloging-in-Publication Data

Schmitt, Conrad J.
    Schaum's easy outline of Spanish / Conrad Schmitt. — 2nd ed.
       p.   cm. — (Schaum's easy outline)
    Includes index.
    ISBN 0-07-176056-3 (alk. paper)
    1. Spanish language—Textbooks for foreign speakers—English.   2. Spanish
language—Grammar. I. Title. II. Title: Easy outline of Spanish.

    PC4129.E5S36   2011
    468.2'421—dc22   2010039820

McGraw-Hill books are available at special quantity discounts to use as premiums and sales promotions or for use in corporate training programs. To contact a representative, please e-mail us at bulksales@mcgraw-hill.com.

This book is printed on acid-free paper.

Contents

Chapter 1
NOUNS AND ARTICLES

IN THIS CHAPTER:

✔ *Noun Endings*
✔ *Nouns That Change Gender*
✔ *Compound Nouns*
✔ *Suffixes*
✔ *Plural Forms of Nouns*
✔ *The Definite Article*
✔ *Indefinite Articles*

Noun Endings

Noun Endings in *-o* and *-a:* Singular Forms Every Spanish noun has a gender, either masculine or feminine. Those nouns that refer to a male, such as *father*, *brother*, etc., are masculine. Those nouns that refer to a female such as *mother*, *sister*, etc., are feminine. For all other nouns, you must learn the gender. You can identify the gender of most Spanish nouns by their endings.

Nouns That End in -*o* These are masculine, with few exceptions.

el muchacho	*boy*
el hermano	*brother*
el gallo	*rooster*
el museo	*museum*
el libro	*book*

Exceptions are **la mano**, *hand*, and a few shortened forms like **la foto** (from **fotografía**), *photograph*.

Nouns That End in -*a* These are generally feminine.

la muchacha	*girl*
la hermana	*sister*
la gallina	*hen*
la montaña	*mountain*
la escuela	*school*

There are two large categories of words that end in **-a** that are exceptions:

Nouns Ending in -*a* That Are Masculine Most are derived from Greek roots.

el día	*day*
el mapa	*map*
el programa	*program*
el clima	*climate*
el tema	*theme*

Nouns Ending in -*ista* Nouns ending in **-ista** refer to professions or political persuasions. They are masculine when referring to a man and feminine when referring to a woman.

el dentista	la dentista
el novelista	la novelista
el comunista	la comunista

Feminine Endings Besides -*a* All nouns ending in **-dad, -tad, -tud, -umbre, -ción, -sión** are feminine.

la ciu<u>dad</u>	*city*
la dificul<u>tad</u>	*difficulty*
la acti<u>tud</u>	*attitude*
la muched<u>umbre</u>	*crowd*
la na<u>ción</u>	*nation*
la inver<u>sión</u>	*investment*

Nouns Ending in -*e* Most nouns ending in **-e** that do not refer to human beings are masculine, but their gender is not predictable.

el parque	*park*
el coche	*car*
el café	*coffee, cafe*
el aire	*air*
el accidente	*accident*

Below is a list of common nouns that end in **-e** but are feminine.

la calle	*street*
la llave	*key*
la clase	*class*
la noche	*night*
la gente	*people*
la parte	*part*
la tarde	*afternoon*

Nouns ending in -*nte* These nouns usually refer to people, and they can be used for both genders. Many Spanish speakers change **-nte** to **-nta** when speaking about a female.

el presidente	*president*
la presidente or **la presidenta**	

el asistente	*assistant*
la asistente or **la asistenta**	

La estudiante and **la cantante** do not change, however.

Nouns That Change Gender

A few Spanish nouns change meaning according to gender. Here is a list of common examples.

el cura	*priest*
la cura	*cure*
el corte	*cut*
la corte	*court*
el capital	*capital* (investment)
la capital	*capital* (city)
el orden	*order* (arrangement)
la orden	*order* (command or religious order)
el papa	*pope*
la papa	*potato*
el policía	*police officer*
la policía	*police department*

Compound Nouns

Compound nouns in Spanish are formed by using a verb root, an adjective, or a preposition with a noun to form one word. Such words are always masculine.

el rascacielos	*skyscraper*
el abrelatas	*can opener*
el tocadiscos	*record player*
el guardarropa	*closet*
el parasol	*parasol*

Suffixes

Spanish speakers alter nouns by adding endings to indicate, among other qualities, size or some characteristic associated with size. The endings **-ito** and **-illo**, when added to nouns, form the diminutive of the noun, which may refer to the actual physical size (smallness) or may show some favorable emotional reaction on the part of the speaker.

casa	**cas<u>ita</u>**	*little house*
perro	**perr<u>ito</u>**	*cute little dog*

Diminutive endings vary in different parts of the Spanish-speaking world. Among Cuban speakers the ending **-ico** is common.

If the noun ends in the consonants **-r** or **-n** or the vowel **-e**, the ending is usually **-cito** instead of **-ito**.

el ratón	**el raton<u>cito</u>**	*cute little mouse*
el café	**el cafe<u>cito</u>**	*demitasse of coffee*

Augmentative forms are used less than diminutive forms. Common augmentative endings are **-ón** and **-ote**. These forms can refer to physical size, but they often have an unfavorable meaning.

grande	**el grandote**	*a really big one*

Plural Forms of Nouns

To form the plural of nouns ending in **-o**, **-a**, or **-e**, you add an **-s**.

el libro	**los libros**
la chica	**las chicas**
el coche	**los coches**

Nouns that end in a consonant form the plural by adding **-es**.

la ciudad	**las ciudad<u>es</u>**
el autobús	**los autobus<u>es</u>**

Nouns ending in **-ción** and **-sión** drop the written accent in the plural.

la ocasión	**las ocasiones**
la nación	**las naciones**

1. Complete the following sentences with the correct definite article.

1. _____ abogado trabaja en esta oficina.
2. _____ calidad vale más que _____ cantidad.
3. _____ novelas están en _____ biblioteca.
4. _____ rascacielos está en _____ centro de _____ ciudad.
5. _____ coche está en _____ parque.
6. _____ amistad es importante.
7. _____ programas van a ser interesantes.
8. Voy a comprar _____ abrelatas.
9. _____ nubes están en _____ cielo por _____ noche.
10. _____ productos son del interior del país.
11. _____ ciudad más importante de _____ nación está en _____ costa.
12. No comprendo _____ sistema.
13. _____ tocadiscos no funciona.
14. _____ periodista escribió todos _____ artículos para _____ periódico.
15. No sé de dónde viene _____ muchedumbre.
16. _____ civilización de _____ indios es interesante.

2. Rewrite the following sentences in the plural.

1. La cantidad es enorme.
2. El drama es muy bueno.
3. La ciudad es bonita.
4. La foto es bonita.
5. El coche es moderno.
6. La casa es bonita.
7. El edificio es alto.
8. El presidente es viejo.
9. La amistad es importante.
10. La civilización es antigua.

The Definite Article

The definite article in English is *the*. In Spanish, the definite articles are **el, la, los,** and **las.**

el libro	**los libros**
la pluma	**las plumas**

Feminine nouns beginning with stressed **a-** or **ha-** take the masculine article **el** in the singular but **las** in the plural.

el arma	**las armas**
el agua	**las aguas**
el hacha	**las hachas**

With General or Abstract Nouns The definite article is used with all general or abstract nouns. In English, the definite article is omitted in such cases.

La leche es buena para los niños.
Milk is good for children.

Los perros son animales domésticos.
Dogs are domestic animals.

With Titles The definite article is used with titles like **señor** when talking about someone; it is omitted in direct discourse.

El doctor González es dentista.
Dr. González is a dentist.

La señora Rodríguez es abogada.
Mrs. Rodríguez is a lawyer.

Buenos días, señorita López.
Good morning, Miss López.

¿Cómo está Ud., profesor Hernández?
How are you, Professor Hernández?

With Languages The grammatical rule concerning the use of the definite article with languages is generally as follows: the definite article is used with languages unless the name of the language immediately follows the verb **hablar** or prepositions **de** and **en.**

> **Hablo español.**
> **Tengo un libro de francés.**
> **El libro está escrito en italiano.**
> **El español es un idioma romance.**
> **Hablo muy bien el francés.**
> **Aprendemos el español.**

In present-day speech, however, it is common to omit the article with languages. You will now often hear **Aprendo español.**

With Days of the Week and Seasons When the definite article is used with days of the week, it has a special meaning. In this case, the definite article means *on.* Study the following examples.

> **Lunes es el primer día de la semana.**
> *Monday is the first day of the week.*

> **Vamos de compras el martes.**
> *We are going shopping on Tuesday.*

> **No tenemos clases los sábados.**
> *We don't have classes on Saturdays.*

The definite article is used with seasons only when discussing the season in a general sense.

> **El verano es una estación de calor.**
> *Summer is a hot season.*

Most grammatical rules state that it is necessary to use the definite article after the preposition **en** with seasons. However, in most present-day speech it is common to omit the article. Either of the following examples is correct.

Hace frío en invierno.
Hace frío en el invierno.

With Parts of the Body and Articles of Clothing With parts of the body and articles of clothing, the definite article is used in Spanish with the reflexive pronoun (see page 82). In English, the possessive adjective rather than the definite article is used. Study the following examples.

Ella se lava las manos antes de comer.
She washes her hands before eating.

Después de comer ella se pone la ropa.
After eating she puts on her clothes.

Note also that the noun is often pluralized in English when there is more than one subject. In Spanish, the noun is in the singular. Study the following examples.

Ellos se quitan la chaqueta antes de comer.
They take off their jackets before eating.

Se lavan la cara y las manos.
They wash their faces and hands.

Since each person has only one jacket and one face, the singular rather than the plural form is used in Spanish.

With Weights and Measures Where English uses the indefinite article with quantities, weights, and measures to mean *per* (*They cost two dollars a dozen*), Spanish uses the definite article.

Esta tela cuesta mil pesos el metro.
This material costs a thousand pesos a meter (or *per meter*).

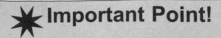

Important Point!

Contractions of the Definite Article

The masculine definite article **el** combines with the prepositions **a** *(to)* and **de** *(of, from, about)* to form one word **al, del.** No contraction is made with **la, los,** or **las.**

Van al mercado.
They are going to the market.

La mayoría del grupo quiere ir.
Most of the group wants to go.

Indefinite Articles

The indefinite articles (English *a, an*) in Spanish are **un** for masculine nouns and **una** for feminine nouns.

> **un libro**
> **un señor**
> **una novela**
> **una señora**

Feminine nouns that begin with a stressed **a-** or **ha-** take the indefinite article **un.**

> **un arma**
> **un hacha**

Plural of the Indefinite Articles The plural forms **unos** and **unas** mean *some* in English. They are often omitted.

> **Compré (unas) flores bonitas.**
> *I bought (some) pretty flowers.*

Omitting the Indefinite Article In Spanish, unlike in English, the indefinite article is omitted after the verb **ser** when it is followed by an unmodified noun. It is used when the noun is modified.

> **El señor López es médico.**
> *Mr. López is a doctor.*
>
> **María es luterana.**
> *Mary is a Lutheran.*
>
> **El señor López es un médico muy bueno.**
> *Mr. López is a very good doctor.*

3. Complete the following sentences with the correct definite or indefinite article when necessary.

1. _____ perros son animales domésticos.
2. _____ carbón es _____ mineral importante.
3. _____ doctor González es _____ cirujano conocido.
4. _____ señora Martín no está aquí.
5. Ellos van a visitar el museo _____ lunes.
6. Él me habla en _____ español.
7. Bueños días, _____ señor López.
8. _____ oro es _____ metal precioso.
9. Ellos siempre están aquí _____ martes.
10. _____ profesor de _____ inglés habla _____ francés también.
11. _____ señora Iglesias es _____ abogada.
12. _____ ciencias son importantes.
13. _____ águila tiene _____ ala rota.
14. _____ hadas son ficticias.

Chapter 2
ADJECTIVES
AND ADVERBS

IN THIS CHAPTER:

✔ *Adjective Endings*
✔ *Comparison and Superlatives*
✔ *Possessive Adjectives*
✔ *Demonstrative Adjectives*
✔ *Exclamatory Expressions*
✔ *Numbers and Numerical Adjectives*

Adjective Endings

Adjectives are words that accompany nouns and add qualities or limit their meaning (*a modern market, this market*). In Spanish, descriptive adjectives usually follow the noun: **un mercado moderno.**

Adjectives Ending in -*o* It is customary to list adjectives in dictionaries in the masculine singular form. Many Spanish adjectives end in **-o** in the masculine singular. Adjectives must agree (i.e., have the same gender and number indicators) with the nouns that they modify. Adjectives that end in **-o** have four possible endings (**-o, -os, -a, -as**).

el mercado moderno	los mercados modernos
la casa moderna	las casas modernas
el puente bonito	los puentes bonitos
la fuente bonita	las fuentes bonitas

Adjectives Ending in -*e* These adjectives have two forms, singular and plural. To form the plural, an **-s** is added.

el campo grande	los campos grandes
la casa grande	las casas grandes

Adjectives Ending in Consonants Most adjectives ending in a consonant have two forms, the singular and the plural. To form the plural, **-es** is added.

el chico popular	los chicos populares
la chica popular	las chicas populares

Adjectives of Nationality Adjectives of nationality that end in **-o** function the same as any regular **-o** adjective.

el mercado mexicano	los mercados mexicanos
la ciudad mexicana	las ciudades mexicanas

Many adjectives of nationality end in a consonant. Unlike regular adjectives ending in a consonant, they have four forms because they add an **-a** to the feminine singular (plural **-as**).

un señor inglés	unos señores ingleses
una señora inglesa	unas señoras inglesas

Special Adjectives Ending in a Consonant Adjectives ending in **-án**, **-ín**, **-ón**, and **-or** follow the same pattern as adjectives of nationality ending in a consonant.

un señor holgazán	*a lazy man*
una senora holgazana	*a lazy woman*
esos señores holgazanes	*those lazy men*
esas señoras holgazanas	*those lazy women*

Exceptions are the adjectives **anterior, exterior, inferior, mejor, peor, posterior, superior,** and **ulterior,** which have only two forms. **Superior** takes an **-a** in the expression **la madre superiora** *(Mother Superior).*

las partes exteriores

Apocopated Adjectives Several adjectives have an apocopated (shortened) form before a masculine singular noun. These adjectives are **bueno, malo, primero, tercero, alguno,** and **ninguno.**

un buen chico
un mal chico
el primer señor
el tercer libro

The adjectives **alguno** and **ninguno** carry a written accent in the shortened form. All other forms of these adjectives are regular.

algún dinero	*some money*
ningún talento	*no talent*

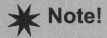

✴ Note!

The adjective **grande** becomes **gran** when used before (but not after) both masculine and feminine singular nouns. It conveys the meaning of *famous* or *great* rather than *big* or *large.*

un gran hombre	*a great man*
una gran mujer	*a famous woman*

The number **ciento**, 100, becomes **cien** before both masculine and feminine nouns.

cien libros   **cien páginas**

Adjectives of Color The words used to express colors in Spanish can be divided into two groups. The meaning of certain words such as **blanco, gris, verde, rojo, amarillo, azul** is the color itself. Since these words are adjectives, they agree with the noun they modify—the same as any other adjective.

la casa blanca	*the white house*
el cielo azul	*the blue sky*

However, many words used in Spanish to express colors refer to something else such as a flower, fruit, or mineral and convey the meaning of the color of the flower, fruit, or mineral. Study the following examples.

	Meaning	*Color*
naranja	*orange*	*orange*
café	*coffee*	*light tan*
marrón	*chestnut*	*brown*
rosa	*rose*	*pink*
vino	*wine*	*reddish purple*
violeta	*violet*	*purple*

Such words as those listed above can be used with the expression **(de) color (de)**. Note too that with each of these prepositions **de** is optional. One could say any of the following.

flores de color de rosa
flores de color rosa } **flores rosa**
flores color de rosa *pink flowers*

Note that these words do not agree with the noun they modify. They are invariable. This means they do not change according to number and gender. However, **marrón** will sometimes agree in the plural: **zapatos marrón(es).**

When a color is modified by another word (English *navy blue, light blue, dark blue* or *bright blue*), it does not agree with the noun it modifies in either gender or number.

una blusa azul oscuro	*a dark blue blouse*
pantalones azul oscuro	*dark blue (navy) pants*

Comparison and Superlatives

Comparison To make the comparative of adjectives (English *more intelligent, taller*), Spanish uses the construction **más... que**.

> **Carlos es más alto que Enrique.**
> *Charles is taller than Henry.*

> **Elena es más inteligente que su hermana.**
> *Helen is more intelligent than her sister.*

This construction can also be used with nouns and adverbs.

> **Yo tengo más dinero que él.**
> *I have more money than he.*

> **El avión va más rápido que el tren.**
> *The plane goes more rapidly than the train.*

When the comparative is followed by a number, **más de** rather than **más que** is used.

> **Tengo más de dos dólares.**

When the sentence is in the negative, **más que** and not **más de** is used with numbers.

> **Ellos no tienen más que cincuenta pesos.**

Superlative of Adjectives The superlative (English *most intelligent, tallest*) is formed by using the word **más** and the appropriate definite article. The superlative expression is followed by the word **de**.

> **Juan es el (chico) más inteligente de la clase.**
> *John is the most intelligent (boy) in the class.*

> **Carlos y Juan son los más altos de la familia.**
> *Charles and John are the tallest in the family.*

Irregular Comparative and Superlative Forms The adjectives **bueno, malo, grande,** and **pequeño** have irregular forms for the comparative and superlative.

bueno	*good*	**mejor**	*better*
malo	*bad*	**peor**	*worse*
grande	*great, big*	**mayor**	*greater, older*
pequeño	*small*	**menor**	*smaller, younger*

In comparisons, Spanish uses these words without the article. For the superlative, it adds the article.

Este libro es mejor (peor) que el otro.
This book is better (worse) than the other.

Este libro es el mejor (peor) de todos.
This book is the best (worst) of all.

With people, **mayor** and **menor** refer to age rather than size.

Juan es mayor que su hermano.
John is older than his brother.

María es la menor de la familia.
Mary is the youngest in the family.

In order to convey the meaning of size, **grande** and **pequeño** are used.

Este perro es más grande que el otro.
This dog is bigger than the other.

Carlos es el más pequeño de la familia.
Charles is the smallest in the family.

Adjectives with -ísimo The suffix **-ísimo** can be added to adjectives to give a superlative connotation (English *most holy, absolutely beautiful*). It gives to the adjective the meaning *most, very, extremely.*

guapo	*handsome*	**guapísimo**	*very handsome*
alta	*tall*	**altísima**	*extremely tall*

Comparisons of Equality The comparison of equality means that two items being compared have equal characteristics (English *She is as clever as her sister*). In Spanish the words **tan... como** are used.

Juan es tan guapo como su hermano.
John is as handsome as his brother.

Estas sillas son tan cómodas como las otras.
These chairs are as comfortable as the others.

Comparisons of Equality with Nouns The comparative of equality can also be expressed with nouns *(as much . . . as, as many . . . as)*. Spanish uses **tanto... como**. The word **tanto** agrees with the noun it modifies.

Carlos tiene tanto dinero como María.
Charles has as much money as Mary.

Ella tiene tanta paciencia como él.
She has as much patience as he (does).

Esta biblioteca tiene tantos libros como la otra.
This library has as many books as the other.

Possessive Adjectives

Possessive adjectives are used to denote ownership or possession. The possessive adjectives **mi** *(my)*, **tu** *(your)*, and **su** *(your, his, her, their)* have only two forms, singular and plural.

mi libro	**mis libros**
mi camisa	**mis camisas**

tu sombrero	**tus sombreros**
tu blusa	**tus blusas**
su coche	**sus coches**
su casa	**sus casas**

Although **su** can mean *his, her, their,* or *your* (formal), the exact meaning is usually clear from the context of the sentence.

María busca su cuaderno.
Mary is looking for her notebook.

If the meaning is not clear from the context of the sentence, a prepositional phrase is used.

María busca el cuaderno de él.
Mary is looking for his notebook.

Below are the possible phrases that can be made from the adjective **su.**

su sombrero	*el sombrero de María, el sombrero de Juan, el sombrero de ella, el sombrero de él, el sombrero de Ud.*
su revista	*la revista de María y Elena, la revista de Juan y Jorge, la revista de ellas, la revista de ellos, la revista de Uds.*

The possessive adjective **nuestro** *(our)* has four forms.

nuestro coche	**nuestros coches**
nuestra casa	**nuestras casas**

The possessive adjective **vuestro** *(your)* also has four forms. This adjective is used only in Spain, where it refers to the **vosotros** subject used in addressing two or more friends. This form is not used in the Latin American countries.

Demonstrative Adjectives

The demonstrative adjective *this* in Spanish is **este** (masculine singular). It has four forms.

este vaso	**estos vasos**
esta mesa	**estas mesas**

In Spanish there are two ways to say *that*. **Ese** is used when the object is near the person spoken to but not the speaker.

Ese libro que Ud. tiene es interesante.
That book that you have is interesting.

Aquel is used when the object is far from both the speaker and the person spoken to.

Aquel libro es interesante.
That book (over there) is interesting.

Ese and **aquel** have four forms.

ese libro	**esos libros**
esa revista	**esas revistas**
aquel pueblo	**aquellos pueblos**
aquella montaña	**aquellas montañas**

Exclamatory Expressions

The exclamation *What a . . . !* in Spanish is expressed by the word **¡Qué!** Note that when the noun is modified the word **más** or **tan** is also used.

¡Qué libro!
What a book!

¡Qué chica más (tan) lista!
What an intelligent girl!

The exclamation *Such a* is expressed by the word **tal.**

| ¡Tal viaje! | *What a trip!* |
| ¡Tal idea! | *Such an idea!* |

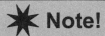

Note!
Formation of Adverbs from Adjectives

Adverbs are formed in Spanish by adding **-mente** to the feminine form of the adjective.

maravillosa	maravillosamente	*marvelously*
enorme	enormemente	*enormously*
fácil	fácilmente	*easily*

Numbers and Numerical Adjectives

Cardinal Numbers

1 uno	11 once	21 veintiuno
2 dos	12 doce	22 veintidós
3 tres	13 trece	23 veintitrés
4 cuatro	14 catorce	24 veinticuatro
5 cinco	15 quince	25 veinticinco
6 seis	16 dieciséis	26 veintiséis
7 siete	17 diecisiete	27 veintisiete
8 ocho	18 dieciocho	28 veintiocho
9 nueve	19 diecinueve	29 veintinueve
10 diez	20 veinte	30 treinta

The numbers 16 through 29 are usually written as one word. Compound numbers from 31 to 99 are written as two words.

31 treinta y uno
42 cuarenta y dos

53 cincuenta y tres
64 sesenta y cuatro
75 setenta y cinco
86 ochenta y seis
97 noventa y siete

The compounds of **ciento,** 100, are regular except for **quinientos, setecientos,** and **novecientos.**

100	ciento (cien)	600	seiscientos
200	doscientos	700	setecientos
300	trescientos	800	ochocientos
400	cuatrocientos	900	novecientos
500	quinientos	1000	mil

Note that **y** *(and)* is used between the tens and unit digits, not between hundreds and tens, as in English *one hundred and thirty-four.*

134 ciento treinta y cuatro
255 doscientos cincuenta y cinco
568 quinientos sesenta y ocho
789 setecientos ochenta y nueve
999 novecientos noventa y nueve

The word **mil** is never preceded by **un.** When preceded by another number such as **dos** or **tres, mil** is not pluralized—**dos mil. tres mil.** It is pluralized in the expression **miles de** *(thousands of).*

Tengo mil dólares.
I have a thousand (one thousand) dollars.

1000	mil	*a thousand (one thousand)*
2000	dos mil	*two thousand*
1011	mil once	*one thousand eleven*

As in English, the article **un** is used with **millón.** The word **millón** is also pluralized.

un millón	*a million (one million)*
dos millones	*two million*

Ordinal Numbers

primero	sexto
segundo	séptimo
tercero	octavo
cuarto	noveno
quinto	décimo

In Spanish the ordinal numbers beyond the tenth **(décimo)** are seldom used.

Pedro segundo	*Peter II (the Second)*
Carlos quinto	*Charles V (the Fifth)*
Luis catorce	*Louis XIV* (literally, *Louis fourteen*)

Primero and **tercero** are shortened before a masculine singular noun.

el primer libro
el tercer artículo
la primera novela
la tercera página

You Need to Know ✓

Converting Adjectives into Nouns

By using the definite article with the adjective, you can turn the adjective into a noun.

El joven lo sabe.
The young man knows it.

Los pequeños juegan en el parque.
The little children are playing in the park.

1. Complete the following sentences with the correct form of the indicated adjective.

1. La casa es _____ y _____. *(bonito, moderno)*
2. El jardín _____ tiene _____ rosas. *(grande, mucho).*
3. Las camisas _____ están en el guardarropa. *(blanco)*
4. En el mercado _____ venden frutas _____. *(antiguo, tropical)*
5. Madrid es una ciudad _____. *(estupendo)*
6. Algunas lecciones son _____ y otras son _____. *(fácil, difícil)*
7. En _____ restaurante _____ sirven comidas _____. *(aquel, lujoso, delicioso)*
8. _____ señores son _____. *(aquel, alemán)*
9. Las comidas _____ y _____ son _____. *(cubano, español, sabroso)*
10. _____ señores _____ están muy _____. *(aquel, delgado, enfermo)*
11. Los labradores son _____. *(fuerte)*
12. No sé dónde están _____ billetes. *(mi)*
13. Las calles _____ de _____ pueblo son _____. *(estrecho, este, pintoresco)*
14. Roberto es un _____ chico. *(bueno)*
15. _____ novela _____ tiene sólo _____ páginas. *(este, interesante, ciento)*
16. Velázquez fue un _____ pintor _____. *(grande, español)*
17. Las playas más _____ están en la costa _____. *(bonito, oriental)*
18. El vinagre es _____ pero el azúcar es _____. *(amargo, dulce)*
19. Los estudiantes _____ sacan muy _____ notas. *(inteligente, bueno)*
20. Estas frutas son las _____ que hay. *(mejor)*
21. Aquel señor es muy _____ y su mujer es muy _____. *(hablador, holgazán)*
22. _____ padres son _____. *(nuestro, español)*

23. Esta camisa _____ _____ juega bien con los
    pantalones _____. *(azul claro, café)*
24. ¿Has visto el saco _____ que compró Jorge? *(rosa)*
25. Él compró zapatos _____ y calcetines _____.
    (marrón, beige)

2. Rewrite the following sentences in the plural.

1. Esta novela es mejor que la otra.
2. El señor argentino habla del gran autor.
3. Esta señora alta es inglesa.
4. Aquel monte está cubierto de nieve.
5. Este chico es más alto y fuerte que aquel chico.
6. Esta niña es la menor de la familia.
7. Este artículo es tan interesante como el otro.
8. El campo verde está en la región occidental.

3. Answer the following questions according to the indicated
response.

1. ¿Quién es más alto, Juan o Roberto? *(Juan)*
2. ¿Cuál es la ciudad más grande del mundo? *(Changhai)*
3. ¿Quién tiene tanto dinero como Roberto? *(Elena)*
4. ¿Quién es la más inteligente de la clase? *(Teresa)*
5. ¿Cuál es el río más largo de los Estados Unidos? *(el Misisipí)*
6. ¿Qué pueblo tiene tantos habitantes como Riobomba? *(Tulúa)*
7. ¿Qué señores tienen la finca? *(Aquel)*
8. ¿Quién tiene mis libros? *(Juan)*
9. ¿Dónde están las fotografías de Juan? *(en la maleta)*
10. ¿Quién es tan bonita como Elena? *(Teresa)*

Chapter 3
VERBS

IN THIS CHAPTER:

✔ Differences between English and Spanish Verbs

✔ Present Tense

✔ Imperfect Tense

✔ Preterite Tense

✔ Future Tense

✔ Conditional Tense

✔ Compound Tenses

✔ The Subjunctive

✔ The Imperative

✔ The Present Participle

✔ Progressive Tenses

✔ Reflexive Verbs

✔ Special Uses of the Infinitive

✔ Passive Voice

Differences between English and Spanish Verbs

Spanish verbs at first appear to be quite difficult to the speaker of English. The reason for this is that Spanish verbs function in quite a different way from English verbs. In English, we use subject pronouns such as *I, you, he*. In Spanish, subject pronouns are relatively unimportant. It is the ending of the verb that indicates the docr of the action. In order to form tenses English verbs use helping verbs as tense indicators. Examples of such auxiliary verbs are *have, had, was, will, would*. In Spanish it is the verb ending that changes in order to indicate the tense of the verb.

Fortunately, each verb does not function as an entity unto itself. Many verbs that are formed in the same way can be grouped together into classes or conjugations. This greatly facilitates learning the verbs. As you will observe in subsequent parts of this chapter, even many so-called irregular verbs have characteristics in common and can thus be grouped together.

Formal Versus Familiar Forms

In Spanish, there are four ways to express the pronoun *you*. When addressing a friend, relative, or close associate the pronoun **tú** is used. This is called the familiar singular form. When addressing someone whom you do not know well, or someone older than yourself, the pronoun **Ud.** (abbreviation for **usted**) is used. This is called the formal singular. When addressing two or more people, either friends or mere acquaintances, the pronoun **Uds.** (abbreviation for **ustedes**) is used. **Uds.** is used as the plural for both the familiar **tú** and the formal **Ud.** You will note, however, that the pronoun **vosotros** does exist. This is the familiar plural of **tú** but its everyday usage is restricted to areas of Spain.

El voseo

The pronoun **vos** is used in familiar speech in many areas of Latin America instead of **tú**. This phenomenon is referred to as **el voseo**. In some areas **el voseo** is used by speakers from all social and educational levels. In other areas it is considered popular. The use of **vos** will be heard in varying degrees in the following areas: Argentina, Uruguay, Paraguay, Chile, Bolivia, parts of Peru, Ecuador, Colombia (excluding the northern coast), parts of Venezuela and Panama, Costa Rica, Nicaragua, El Salvador, Honduras, Guatemala, the state of Chiapas in Mexico, and in a very small area of Cuba.

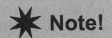

✳ Note!

Verbal Object Indicator

When a direct object of a verb is a person, it is preceded by **a** in Spanish. The **a** is not translated into English.

Veo a Juan.	*I see John.*
Miramos al niño.	*We're looking at the little boy.*

Present Tense

Regular First Conjugation Verbs The **-ar** verbs are referred to as first conjugations verbs. Their infinitive (**hablar, mirar, estudiar**) ends in **-ar.**

In order to form the present tense of **-ar** verbs, you drop the infinitive ending **-ar** and add the personal endings **-o, -as, -a, -amos, -áis, -an** to what remains (the root or stem).

Infinitive	preparar	hablar	Endings
Root	prepar-	habl-	
yo	preparo	hablo	-o
tú	preparas	hablas	-as
él			
ella }	prepara	habla	-a
Ud.			

nosotros(as)	preparamos	hablamos	-amos
vosotros(as)	preparáis	habláis	-áis
ellos ellas Uds. }	preparan	hablan	-an

Yo trabajo mucho.	Nosotros estudiamos.
Tú cantas bien	Vosotras viajáis.
Él habla español.	Ustedes bailan bien.
Ud. gana bastante.	Ellos(as) nadan.

Ir, dar, estar The verbs **ir, dar,** and **estar** are considered irregular in the present tense. You will note, however, that the only irregularity exists in the first person singular **(yo).** All other forms are the same as those for a regular **-ar** verb.

ir	dar	estar
voy	doy	estoy
vas	das	estás
va	da	está
vamos	damos	estamos
vais	dais	estáis
van	dan	están

Regular Second Conjugation Verbs In order to form the present tense of regular **-er** verbs, drop the infinitive ending and add the personal endings **-o, -es, -e, -emos, -éis, -en.**

Infinitive Root	comer com-	vender vend-	Endings
yo	como	vendo	-o
tú	comes	vendes	-es
él, ella, Ud.	come	vende	-e
nosotros(as)	comemos	vendemos	-emos
vosotros(as)	coméis	vendéis	-éis
ellos(as), Uds.	comen	venden	-en

The verb **ver** *(to see)* has an irregular first person singular: **veo.**

Regular Third Conjugation Verbs The infinitives of regular third conjugation verbs end in **-ir**. To form the present tense, drop the infinitive ending **-ir** and add the personal endings **-o, -es, -e, -imos, -ís, -en** to the root.

Infinitive	abrir	vivir	Endings
Root	abr-	viv-	
yo	abro	vivo	-o
tú	abres	vives	-es
él, ella, Ud.	abre	vive	-e
nosotros(as)	abrimos	vivimos	-imos
vosotros(as)	abrís	vivís	-ís
ellos(as), Uds.	abren	viven	-en

The endings are the same for the second (**-er**) and third (**-ir**) conjugation verbs except in the **nosotros** and **vosotros** forms.

Volvemos a México.
Vivimos en México.

Irregular Verbs *poner, hacer, valer, traer, salir* These verbs have irregular forms in the first person singular (**yo**): **pongo, hago, valgo, traigo, salgo.** All other forms are regular and the personal endings are either those of **-er** or **-ir** verbs, depending upon the conjugation to which the verb belongs.

	hacer	salir
yo	hago	salgo
tú	haces	sales
él, ella, Ud.	hace	sale
nosotros(as)	hacemos	salimos
vosotros(as)	hacéis	salís
ellos(as), Uds.	hacen	salen

Aparecer, conocer, ofrecer, conducir, producir, traducir Most verbs that end in **-cer** or **-cir** are also irregular in the first person singular: **aparezco, conozco, ofrezco, conduzco, produzco, traduzco.** All other forms are regular.

parecer	reducir
parezco	reduzco
pareces	reduces
parece	reduce
parecemos	reducimos
parecéis	reducís
parecen	reducen

> **Ser** The verb **ser**, *to be,* is irregular in the present tense. No other verb follows the same pattern:
>
> | soy | somos |
> |-----|-------|
> | eres | sois |
> | es | son |

Saber The verb *to know* is irregular in the first person singular of the present tense: **sé, sabes, sabe, sabemos, sabéis, saben.**

First Class Stem-changing Verbs Verbs that have changes in the stem are grouped into three classes or patterns. Verbs of the first class are **-ar** and **-er** verbs that have an **-e-** in the stem that changes to **-ie-** when stressed, or an **-o-** that changes to **-ue-**. In other words, the change occurs in all forms except **nosotros** and **vosotros**. Some important verbs of this class are:

e - ie		o - ue	
cerrar	*to close*	acordar	*to remember*
comenzar	*to begin, start*	almorzar	*to have lunch*
defender	*to defend*	contar	*to tell, count*
despertar	*to awaken*	costar	*to cost*
empezar	*to begin*	encontrar	*to meet, find*
entender	*to understand*	mostrar	*to show*
negar	*to deny*	probar	*to prove*
pensar	*to think*	recordar	*to remember*
perder	*to lose*	devolver	*to give back*
querer	*to want*	envolver	*to wrap*
		mover	*to move*
		poder	*to be able*
		volver	*to return*

cerrar	querer	contar	poder
cierro	quiero	cuento	puedo
cierras	quieres	cuentas	puedes
cierra	quiere	cuenta	puede
cerramos	queremos	contamos	podemos
cerráis	queréis	contáis	podéis
cierran	quieren	cuentan	pueden

The verb **jugar** also has a stem change.

juego, juegas, juega, jugamos, jugáis, juegan

Tener and *venir* The verbs **tener** *(to have)* and **venir** *(to come)* are stem-changing verbs in the present tense. In addition, the first person singular is irregular.

tener	venir
tengo	vengo
tienes	vienes
tiene	viene
tenemos	venimos
tenéis	venís
tienen	vienen

Second Class Stem-changing Verbs: *e - ie o - ue* Second class stem-changing verbs change the infinitive stem **-e-** to **-ie-** or the infinitive stem **-o-** to **-ue-** in all forms except **nosotros** (and **vosotros**). Some important verbs of this class are:

mentir	*to lie*	sugerir	*to suggest*
preferir	*to prefer*	dormir	*to sleep*
sentir	*to regret*	morir	*to die*

preferir	sentir	dormir
prefiero	siento	duermo
prefieres	sientes	duermes
prefiere	siente	duerme
preferimos	sentimos	dormimos
preferís	sentís	dormís
prefieren	sienten	duermen

You will note that in the present tense these changes are the same as those of the first class stem-changing verbs. For the verbs of the second class, however, there will be changes in other tenses. For this reason they are grouped separately.

Third Class Stem-changing Verbs: *e - i* The third class of stem-changing verbs are those which change the **-e-** of the stem to **-i-** in all forms of the present tense except **nosotros** and **vosotros**. Verbs that belong to this class are:

despedir	*to dismiss, fire*	**reír**	*to laugh*
freír	*to fry*	**reñir**	*to argue*
impedir	*to impede*	**repetir**	*to repeat*
medir	*to measure*	**servir**	*to serve*
pedir	*to ask for*	**sonreír**	*to smile*

pedir	**repetir**	**reír**
pido	repito	río
pides	repites	ríes
pide	repite	ríe
pedimos	repetimos	reímos
pedís	repetís	reís
piden	repiten	ríen

The verbs **seguir** *(to follow)*, **conseguir** *(to get)*, and **perseguir** *(to follow after)* also belong to the third class stem-changing verbs. Note the spelling pattern **-go -gue -gui-**.

  sigo, sigues, sigue, seguimos, seguís, siguen

Decir The verb **decir** *(to say),* in the present tense, has the same stem change as **e - i** verbs, and the first person singular (**yo**) is irregular.

  digo, dices, dice, decimos, decís, dicen

Verbs Ending in -*uir* Infinitives that end in **-uir** insert a **-y-** in all forms of the present except **nosotros** and **vosotros**.

construir	huir
construyo	huyo
construyes	huyes
construye	huye
construimos	huimos
construís	huís
construyen	huyen

The verb **oír** *(to hear)* is conjugated in the same way, with the exception of the first person singular **(yo)**.

oigo, oyes, oye, oímos, oís, oyen

Special Uses of the Present Tense The expression **hace** or **desde hace** is used with a verb in the present tense to indicate an action that began in the past and continues into the present.

Hace un año que estoy en México.
I have been in Mexico for a year.

Estoy en México desde hace un año.
I have been in Mexico for a year.

¿Cuánto tiempo hace que Ud. está en México?
How long have you been in Mexico?

You Need to Know ✓

The expression **por poco** is used with a verb in the present tense to express what almost happened. In English the past tense is used to convey this idea.

Por poco perdemos el autobús.
We almost missed the bus.

1. Complete the following sentences with the correct form of the present tense of the indicated verb.
    1. Yo _____ a María. *(conocer)*
    2. Ellos _____ buena comida en aquel restaurante. *(servir)*
    3. Nosotros _____ en la capital. *(vivir)*
    4. Nosotros _____ muy bien el español. *(hablar)*
    5. Aquel niño _____ mucho. *(comer)*
    6. Yo _____ cada mañana a las ocho. *(salir)*
    7. Uds. _____ muchos viajes. *(hacer)*
    8. Él _____ viajar en avión. *(preferir)*
    9. Nosotros no _____ ningún favor. *(pedir)*
    10. ¿Qué _____ los ingenieros? *(construir)*
    11. ¿A qué hora _____ tú? *(volver)*
    12. Nosotros no _____ terminar el trabajo. *(poder)*
    13. Yo no _____ nada. *(oír)*
    14. Él _____ que todo _____ mucho. *(decir, costar)*
    15. Nosotros _____ que él _____ bien. *(saber, jugar)*
    16. Yo lo _____ en el sobre y luego lo _____ por correo. *(poner, mandar)*
    17. Yo _____ de la oficina y luego tú _____ a la fábrica. *(venir, ir)*
    18. Yo no _____ lo que _____ él. *(saber, decir)*
    19. Nosotros _____ en la planta baja. *(vivir)*
    20. Ellos siempre _____ en el verano. *(nadar)*
    21. Yo _____ que yo _____ que yo lo _____. *(decir, saber, conocer)*
    22. Ellos lo _____ hacer si _____. *(poder, querer)*
    23. Yo _____ que _____ ingeniero. *(repetir, ser)*
    24. Ella _____ que ella _____ que ellos _____ en España. *(decir, saber, estar)*

2. Complete the following sentences with the correct form of the indicated verb.
    1. Hace casi un día entero que nosotros _____ aquí en el aeropuerto. *(estar)*
    2. Hace a lo menos once horas que no _____ ningún avión. *(llegar)*
    3. Y hace ocho horas que no _____ ningún vuelo. *(salir)*
    4. Por poco me _____ de hambre. *(morir)*

Imperfect Tense

Regular *-ar* Verbs In order to form the imperfect tense of regular **-ar** verbs, you drop the infinitive ending **-ar** and add the following endings: **-aba, -abas, -aba, -ábamos, -abais, -aban.**

Infinitive	hablar	mirar	Endings
Root	habl-	mir-	
yo	hablaba	miraba	-aba
tú	hablabas	mirabas	-abas
él, ella, Ud.	hablaba	miraba	-aba
nosotros(as)	hablábamos	mirábamos	-ábamos
vosotros(as)	hablabais	mirabais	-abais
ellos(as), Uds.	hablaban	miraban	-aban

Regular *-er* and *-ir* Verbs The endings for the imperfect tense of regular second and third conjugation verbs (**-er, -ir**) are the same. You drop the infinitive ending and add the following: **-ía, -ías, -ía, -íamos, -íais, -ían.**

Infinitive	comer	vivir	Endings
Root	com-	viv-	
yo	comía	vivía	-ía
tú	comías	vivías	-ías
él, ella, Ud.	comía	vivía	-ía
nosotros(as)	comíamos	vivíamos	-íamos
vosotros(as)	comíais	vivíais	-íais
ellos(as), Uds.	comían	vivían	-ían

Irregular Verbs There are only three irregular verbs in the imperfect tense. They are **ir, ser,** and **ver.**

Infinitive	ir	ser	ver
yo	iba	era	veía
tú	ibas	eras	veías
él, ella, Ud.	iba	era	veía
nosotros(as)	íbamos	éramos	veíamos
vosotros(as)	ibais	erais	veíais
ellos(as), Uds.	iban	eran	veían

Uses of the Imperfect Tense

Continuing Action The imperfect tense is used to express continuing actions, or repeated actions in the past that are either customary or habitual. Some common adverbial expressions that indicate continuance and are frequently used with the imperfect tense are:

siempre	*always*
con frecuencia	*frequently*
frecuentemente	*frequently*
a menudo	*often*
a veces	*sometimes*
de vez en cuando	*from time to time*
muchas veces	*often*
cada año (día, mes)	*every year (day, month)*
todos los días	*every day*
los jueves	*on Thursdays*

Ellos siempre hablaban español.
Él venía aquí con frecuencia.
Yo visitaba a mis amigos a menudo.
Ellos comían allí de vez en cuando.
Íbamos muchas veces a México.
Él viajaba cada verano.
Ellos volvían todos los días a la misma hora.

Mental Activity

Since most mental processes involve duration or continuance, verbs that deal with mental processes are often expressed in the imperfect tense. Common verbs of this nature are **querer** *(to want)*, **sentir** *(to be sorry)*, **pensar** *(to think)*, **saber** *(to know)*, **creer** *(to believe)*.

Description in the Past The imperfect tense is used to express description in the past.

> Hacía buen tiempo.
> El niño tenía sueño.
> Él era rubio.
> Eran las seis de la noche.

With the Time Expression *hacía* The imperfect tense is used with the time expression **hacía**. In English the pluperfect tense is used.

> **Hacía cinco años que ellos estaban en Chile.**
> *They had been in Chile for five years.*

> **Hacía un año que nosotros lo sabíamos.**
> *We had known it for a year.*

3. Complete the following descriptive passage with the correct form of the imperfect of the indicated verbs.

El señor _____ *(estar)* en la ciudad. Pero él no _____ *(ser)* de la ciudad. _____ *(ser)* de un pueblo pequeño que _____ *(quedar)* a unos cien kilómetros de la ciudad. El señor _____ *(tener)* unos veinte años. _____ *(ser)* alto y delgado y _____ *(tener)* los ojos azules y el pelo castaño. El pobre _____ *(estar)* cansado y triste porque _____ *(trabajar)* mucho y se _____ *(encontrar)* lejos de su familia y de sus queridos. Él _____ *(tener)* ganas de volver a casa. _____ *(querer)* descansar y ver a su familia pero no _____ *(poder)* porque _____ *(tener)* que seguir trabajando. Su familia _____ *(necesitar)* el dinero que él _____ *(ganar)* y que les _____ *(mandar)* cada semana.

_____ *(ser)* las once de la noche y él _____ *(estar)* en la cama pero no _____ *(poder)* conciliar el sueño. Él _____ *(tener)* frío porque afuera _____ *(hacer)* frío y _____ *(nevar)*. El pobre señor no _____ *(tener)* suficiente dinero para comprarse una manta y el cuarto humilde que _____ *(alquilar)* no _____ *(tener)* calefacción.

Preterite Tense

The preterite is the past tense used to express an action completed at a definite time in the past.

Regular -ar Verbs Drop the infinitive ending **-ar** and add the personal endings **-é, -aste, -ó, -amos, -asteis, -aron.**

Infinitive	hablar	mirar	Endings
Root	habl-	mir-	
yo	hablé	miré	-é
tú	hablaste	miraste	-aste
él, ella, Ud.	habló	miró	-ó
nosotros(as)	hablamos	miramos	-amos
vosotros(as)	hablasteis	mirasteis	-asteis
ellos(as), Uds.	hablaron	miraron	-aron

Because of the spelling patterns **ca, que, qui, co, cu; ga, gue, gui, go, gu; za, ce, ci, zo, zu,** the following verbs have special spellings. Note the following examples.

buscar	jugar	empezar
busqué	jugué	empecé
buscaste	jugaste	empezaste
buscó	jugó	empezó
buscamos	jugamos	empezamos
buscasteis	jugasteis	empezasteis
buscaron	jugaron	empezaron

Regular -er and -ir Verbs To form the preterite of regular **-er** and **-ir** verbs, drop the infinitive ending **-er** or **-ir** and add the personal endings **-í, iste, ió, -imos, -isteis, -ieron.**

Infinitive	comer	vivir	Endings
Root	com-	viv-	
yo	comí	viví	-í
tú	comiste	viviste	-iste
él, ella, Ud.	comió	vivió	-ió

nosotros(as)	comimos	vivimos	-imos
vosotros(as)	comisteis	vivisteis	-isteis
ellos(as), Uds.	comieron	vivieron	-ieron

Remember

The Verb dar

To give is irregular in the preterite. It is conjugated the same as a second or third conjugation verb.

di	dimos
diste	disteis
dio	dieron

Second class Stem-changing Verbs These verbs have a stem change in both the present and the preterite. Verbs like **sentir** *(to feel)* have an **-i-** in the third person singular and plural. Verbs like **dormir** *(to sleep)* have a **-u**.

    sentí, sentiste, sintió, sentimos, sentisteis, sintieron

    dormí, dormiste, durmió, dormimos, dormisteis, durmieron

Third class Stem-changing Verbs The third class stem-changing verbs have an **-i-** in the third person singular and plural forms.

    pedí, pediste, pidió, pedimos, pedisteis, pidieron

Verbs with -y- in the Stem Infinitives that end in **-uir** have a **-y-** in the third person singular and plural endings. The verbs **leer** *(to read)* and **oír** *(to hear)* also belong to this group in the preterite.

contribuir	leer	oír
contribuí	leí	oí
contribuiste	leíste	oíste
contribuyó	leyó	oyó
contribuimos	leímos	oímos
contribuisteis	leísteis	oísteis
contribuyeron	leyeron	oyeron

Irregular Verbs Many common verbs are irregular in the preterite tense. Many irregular verbs can be grouped together because they have the same irregularity in the root and they take the same endings.

Tener *(to have)*, **andar** *(to walk)*, **estar** *(to be)* have **-uv-** in the preterite stem.

tener	andar	estar
tuve	anduve	estuve
tuviste	anduviste	estuviste
tuvo	anduvo	estuvo
tuvimos	anduvimos	estuvimos
tuvisteis	anduvisteis	estuvisteis
tuvieron	anduvieron	estuvieron

Poner *(to put)*, **poder** *(to be able)*, **saber** *(to know)*, **caber** *(to fit)* have a **-u-** in the preterite stem.

poner	poder	saber	caber
puse	pude	supe	cupe
pusiste	pudiste	supiste	cupiste
puso	pudo	supo	cupo
pusimos	pudimos	supimos	cupimos
pusisteis	pudisteis	supisteis	cupisteis
pusieron	pudieron	supieron	cupieron

Querer *(to want)*, **hacer** *(to do)*, **venir** *(to come)* have an **-i-** in the preterite stem.

querer	hacer	venir
quise	hice	vine
quisiste	hiciste	viniste
quiso	hizo	vino
quisimos	hicimos	vinimos
quisisteis	hicisteis	vinisteis
quisieron	hicieron	vinieron

Decir *(to say)*, **traer** *(to carry)*, **producir** *(to produce)*, **traducir** *(to translate)* have a **-j-** in the preterite stem. Note that the third person singular ending is **-o** and the third person plural ending is **-eron**.

decir	traer	traducir
dije	traje	traduje
dijiste	trajiste	tradujiste
dijo	trajo	tradujo
dijimos	trajimos	tradujimos
dijisteis	trajisteis	tradujisteis
dijeron	trajeron	tradujeron

Ir *(to go)* and **ser** *(to be)* have the same forms in the preterite. Meaning is made clear by the context of the sentence.

ir	ser
fui	fui
fuiste	fuiste
fue	fue
fuimos	fuimos
fuisteis	fuisteis
fueron	fueron

4. Complete the following sentences with the correct form of the preterite of the indicated verb.

1. Ellos _____ un viaje. *(hacer)*
2. ¿Por qué no lo _____ tú al inglés? *(traducir)*
3. María no _____ salir. *(querer)*
4. Ellos _____ todo en orden. *(poner)*
5. ¿Dónde _____ Ud.? *(estar)*
6. Ella no _____ las provisiones. *(traer)*
7. Los chicos _____ y ella _____ la guitarra. *(cantar, tocar)*
8. Nosotros _____ a las ocho. *(venir)*
9. Tú no lo _____ hacer. *(poder)*
10. El director me lo _____. *(decir)*

11. Yo no _____ nada del asunto. *(saber)*
12. Juanito lo _____ todo. *(comer)*
13. Ellos no _____ las últimas noticias. *(oír)*
14. Él me _____ un favor. *(pedir)*
15. Nosotros _____ que salir en seguida. *(tener)*

5. Rewrite the following sentences in the preterite.
    1. La compañía no tiene suficientes fondos económicos.
    2. ¿Por qué vienes a las ocho de la mañana?
    3. Él no puede ayudarme.
    4. Tú buscas los informes.
    5. Nosotros andamos por la capital.
    6. ¿Quién te lo dice?
    7. Los alumnos no lo saben.
    8. Yo voy en tren.
    9. Ellos no están aquí.
    10. ¿Por qué no lo ponemos en el garage?
    11. Él no lee el programa del día.
    12. No lo hacemos sin ayuda.

Uses of the Preterite

Completed Past Action The preterite expresses an action that was completed at a definite time in the past. Some common adverbial phrases that often accompany the preterite are:

ayer	*yesterday*
anteayer	*the day before yesterday*
anoche	*last night*
el otro día	*the other day*
hace dos días (años)	*two days (years) ago*
la semana pasada	*last week*
el año pasado	*last year*
durante tres siglos	*for three centuries*

Changes of Meaning in the Preterite Certain common verbs, like **querer** *(to want)*, **poder** *(to be able)*, **saber** *(to know)*, **conocer** *(to know [someone])*, change meaning when used in the preterite.

María no quiso salir.
Mary refused to leave.

Él pudo huir.
He managed to escape.

Carlos no pudo hacerlo.
Charles couldn't do it (but he tried).

Ellos lo supieron ayer.
They found it out yesterday.

Juan conoció a María.
John met Mary.

Differences between Preterite and Imperfect: Completed versus noncompleted action The imperfect expresses a continuing action in the past; the preterite expresses an action begun and completed in the past, even if the action lasted for some time.

Él venía aquí cada día.
Él vino aquí ayer.

Ellos estaban en España por mucho tiempo.
(It is not stated whether or not they are still there.)
Los árabes estuvieron en España por ocho siglos.
(They are no longer there.)

Two actions in one sentence In order to determine the tense of each verb when there is more than one action in a sentence, it is sometimes helpful to think of a stage. Anything that is scenery or that takes place in the background is expressed by the imperfect. Any action that is carried out by the performers on the stage is in the preterite.

Juan entró y María salió.
Llovía cuando ellos salieron.
Los niños jugaban mientras sus
  padres los miraban.

Sometimes the tense will change depending upon the idea that the speaker wishes to convey.

Un señor vendió el carro y el otro lo compró.

In the sentence you just read, the speaker is simply reporting what took place.

Un señor vendía el carro y el otro lo compraba.

In this sentence, the speaker wishes to describe the background, what was taking.

6. Rewrite the following sentences in either the preterite or imperfect, according to the indicated time expression.
   1. Ellos miraron la televisión anoche.

      _____ cada noche.
   2. Juan estuvo aquí ayer.

      _____ el otro día también.
   3. Fuimos allá el año pasado.

      _____ muy a menudo.
   4. Comían en aquel restaurante todos los sábados.

      _____ el sábado pasado.
   5. Yo lo veía de vez en cuando.

      _____ con frecuencia.
   6. Anoche discutimos el mismo problema.

      Siempre _____.
   7. El profesor lo repetía muchas veces.

      _____ una vez.
   8. El director desapareció en 1940.

      _____ de vez en cuando.
   9. Su padre siempre estaba enfermo.

      _____ por tres años.
   10. Durante el último viaje, él pagó con cheques de viajero.

       Durante todos sus viajes, _____.

7. Complete the following sentences with either the preterite or imperfect of the indicated verb.

   1. Unos amigos _____ mientras los otros _____ el sol. *(nadar, tomar)*
   2. María _____ con su madre cuando yo _____. *(hablar, entrar)*
   3. Ellos lo _____ cuando nosotros _____. *(discutir, interrumpir)*
   4. Mi madre _____ la comida mientras mi padre _____ la mesa. *(preparar, poner)*
   5. Yo _____ cuando _____ el teléfono. *(dormir, sonar)*
   6. Ellos _____ cuando yo _____ por teléfono. *(comer, llamar)*
   7. Mis padres _____ la televisión mientras yo _____. *(mirar, estudiar)*
   8. Ellos _____ de las elecciones cuando yo _____ los resultados. *(hablar, anunciar)*
   9. Cuando ellos _____ al aeropuerto, _____ buen tiempo. *(llegar, hacer)*
   10. Unos _____ mientras otros _____. *(bailar, cantar)*

Future Tense

Ir a **with Infinitive** The future can be expressed by using **ir a** *(to be going to)* with an infinitive.

> **Vamos a comer en casa.**
> *We are going to eat at home.*

> **Ellos van a vivir con nosotros.**
> *They are going to live with us.*

Regular Verbs You form the future tense of regular verbs by adding the following endings to the infinitive: **-é, -ás, -á, -emos, -éis, -án.**

Infinitive	**hablar**	**comer**	**escribir**
Root	**habl-**	**com-**	**escrib-**
yo	**hablaré**	**comeré**	**escribiré**
tú	**hablarás**	**comerás**	**escribirás**
él, ella, Ud.	**hablará**	**comerá**	**escribirá**
nosotros(as)	**hablaremos**	**comeremos**	**escribiremos**
vosotros(as)	**hablaréis**	**comeréis**	**escribiréis**
ellos(as), Uds.	**hablarán**	**comerán**	**escribirán**

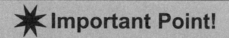

✳Important Point!

Spanish and English speakers use the future tense in much the same way. In everyday conversation **ir a** with the infinitive is more commonly used than the true future.

Irregular Verbs The following verbs have irregular future stems.

decir	**diré**
hacer	**haré**
querer	**querré**
caber	**cabré**
poder	**podré**
saber	**sabré**
poner	**pondré**
salir	**saldré**
tener	**tendré**
valer	**valdré**
venir	**vendré**

decir	poner
diré	pondré
dirás	pondrás
dirá	pondrá
diremos	pondremos
direis	pondreis
dirán	pondrán

8. Complete the following sentences with the correct form of the future of the indicated verb.

1. Carlos _____ el problema con nosotros. *(discutir)*
2. Yo _____ del asunto más tarde. *(hablar)*
3. ¿Cuándo _____ tú aquí? *(estar)*
4. Nosotros no _____ en casa esta noche. *(comer)*
5. Ellos _____ el paquete por correo. *(recibir)*
6. Nosotros _____ pasado mañana. *(volver)*
7. Yo _____ en español. *(cantar)*
8. La familia _____ una casa particular. *(comprar)*
9. Nosotros no _____ todos los libros. *(vender)*
10. El tren _____ a las ocho y cuarto. *(llegar)*

9. Rewrite the following sentences in the future tense.

1. Ellos hacen un viaje.
2. Carlitos no quiere salir.
3. Yo tengo bastante tiempo.
4. ¿Cuánto vale la joya?
5. Nosotros salimos a las ocho en punto.
6. Tú dices la verdad.
7. Uds. vienen en avión, ¿no?
8. Yo sé los resultados.
9. ¿Por qué no puedes jugar?
10. Todos no caben en el mismo carro.

Conditional

Regular Verbs To form the conditional, you add the personal endings to the entire infinitive. The endings are the same as those of the imperfect of second and third conjugation verbs: **-ía, -ías, -ía, -íamos, -íais, -ían.**

Infinitive	**hablar**	**comer**	**vivir**
Root	**habl-**	**com-**	**viv-**
	hablaría	**comería**	**viviría**
	hablarías	**comerías**	**vivirías**
	hablaría	**comería**	**viviría**
	hablaríamos	**comeríamos**	**viviríamos**
	hablaríais	**comeríais**	**viviríais**
	hablarían	**comerían**	**vivirían**

The conditional in Spanish, as in English, expresses what would or would not happen under certain conditions.

Yo iría pero no tengo tiempo.
I would go but I don't have time.

Irregular Verbs The same verbs that are irregular in the future are irregular in the conditional.

decir	**diría**
hacer	**haría**
querer	**querría**
caber	**cabría**
poder	**podría**
saber	**sabría**
poner	**pondría**
salir	**saldría**
tener	**tendría**
valer	**valdría**
venir	**vendría**

Special Uses of the Future and Conditional

The future and conditional tenses are used to express probability. The future expresses a present probable action and the conditional expresses a past probable action.

¿Qué hora será?	*What time can it be?*
Serán las tres.	*It is probably three o'clock.*
¿Qué hora sería?	*What time could it have been?*
Serían las tres.	*It was probably three o'clock.*

10. Complete the following sentences with the correct form of the conditional of the indicated verb.

1. Ellos _____ en el mar pero el agua está fría. *(nadar)*
2. Yo _____ un soneto pero no soy poeta. *(escribir)*
3. Él me _____ pero no tiene el dinero. *(pagar)*
4. Nosotros _____ el carro pero nadie lo quiere. *(vender)*
5. Ellos _____ en la capital pero cuesta demasiado. *(vivir)*

11. Complete the following sentences with the correct form of the conditional of the indicated verb.

1. Yo _____ el viaje con mucho gusto pero la verdad es que no tengo el tiempo. *(hacer)*
2. ¿_____ (tú) bastante dinero para hacer el viaje? *(tener)*
3. Ya lo creo. Yo sé que _____ suficiente dinero. Eso no _____ ningún problema. *(tener, ser)*
4. Y Paco _____ el viaje. *(hacer)*
5. Él ya me dijo que _____ el dinero. *(tener)*
6. Pero (él) nunca _____ el dinero. *(tener)*
7. Nosotros le _____ prestar el dinero. *(poder)*
8. Él nos _____ cada céntimo. *(devolver)*
9. Sí, pero yo lo conozco bien. Él no _____ tomar el dinero. *(querer)*
10. (Eso) le _____ vergüenza. *(dar)*

Compound Tenses

The compound tenses are formed with the appropriate tense of **haber** and the past participle.

Formation of the Past Participle Form the past participle by dropping the infinitive ending (**-ar, -er, -ir**) and adding **-ado** to **-ar** verbs and **-ido** to **-er** and **-ir** verbs.

Infinitive	Past Participle
hablar	**hablado**
comer	**comido**
pedir	**pedido**

The following common verbs have irregular past participles:

abrir	**abierto**
cubrir	**cubierto**
descubrir	**descubierto**
escribir	**escrito**
freír	**frito**
romper	**roto**
ver	**visto**
morir	**muerto**
poner	**puesto**
volver	**vuelto**
decir	**dicho**
hacer	**hecho**

Present Perfect

The present perfect is formed by using the present tense of the verb **haber** with the past participle.

hablar	**comer**	**abrir**
he hablado	**he comido**	**he abierto**
has hablado	**has comido**	**has abierto**
ha hablado	**ha comido**	**ha abierto**

hemos hablado	**hemos comido**	**hemos abierto**
habéis hablado	**habéis comido**	**habéis abierto**
han hablado	**han comido**	**han abierto**

The present perfect tense is used to express a past action without reference to a particular time. It usually denotes an occurrence that continues into the present or relates closely to the present.

Mi abuelo ha estado enfermo.
My grandfather has been ill.

Ellos han llegado hoy.
They have arrived today.

Hemos comido allí.
We have eaten there.

The present perfect is commonly used with the adverb **ya.**

Ya han llegado.   *They have already arrived.*

Pluperfect

The pluperfect is formed by using the imperfect tense of the auxiliary verb **haber** with the past participle.

hablar	comer	escribir
había hablado	**había comido**	**había escrito**
habías hablado	**habías comido**	**habías escrito**
había hablado	**había comido**	**había escrito**
habíamos hablado	**habíamos comido**	**habíamos escrito**
habíais hablado	**habíais comido**	**habíais escrito**
habían hablado	**habían comido**	**habían escrito**

The pluperfect is used the same in Spanish as in English to express a past action completed prior to another past action.

> **Él había hablado y luego nos fuimos.**
> *He had spoken and then we left.*

> **Ellos ya habían terminado cuando yo salí.**
> *They had already finished when I left.*

Preterite Perfect

The preterite perfect is formed by using the preterite of the verb **haber** and the past participle.

> **hube llegado**
> **hubiste llegado**
> **hubo llegado**
> **hubimos llegado**
> **hubisteis llegado**
> **hubieron llegado**

The preterite perfect is used mainly in writing and is always preceded by a time expression such as **en cuanto** *(as soon as)*, **luego que** *(as soon as)*, **apenas** *(scarcely)*, **cuando** *(when)*.

> **Apenas hubieron llegado cuando salieron los otros.**
> *They had scarcely arrived when the others left.*

> **Luego que hubimos comido, empezó la conferencia.**
> *As soon as we had eaten, the lecture began.*

Future Perfect

The future perfect tense is formed by using the future of the auxiliary verb **haber** and the past participle.

hablar	comer	escribir
habré hablado	habré comido	habré escrito
habrás hablado	habrás comido	habrás escrito
habrá hablado	habrá comido	habrá escrito

habremos hablado	habremos comido	habremos escrito
habreis hablado	habreis comido	habreis escrito
habrán hablado	habrán comido	habrán escrito

The future perfect tense is used to express a future action that will be completed prior to another future action. This particular tense is not used often.

Ellos habrán salido antes del concierto.
They will have left before the concert.

Conditional Perfect

The conditional perfect is formed by using the conditional of the auxiliary verb **haber** and the past participle.

jugar	beber	decir
habría jugado	habría bebido	habría dicho
habrías jugado	habrías bebido	habrías dicho
habría jugado	habría bebido	habría dicho
habríamos jugado	habríamos bebido	habríamos dicho
habríais jugado	habríais bebido	habríais dicho
habrían jugado	habrían bebido	habrían dicho

The conditional perfect is used to express what would have taken place had something else not interfered. You will have need to use the conditional perfect much more frequently than the future perfect.

Ellos habrían hecho el viaje pero no tuvieron bastante dinero.
They would have taken the trip but they didn't have enough money.

Él habría venido pero no tenía el coche.
He would have come but he didn't have the car.

12. Complete the following sentences with the correct form of the present perfect of the indicated verb.

1. Ellos _____ aquí. *(estar)*
2. María _____ mi canción favorita. *(cantar)*
3. Hasta ahora él no _____ a mi carta. *(contestar)*
4. ¿_____ Uds. el trabajo? *(empezar)*
5. Yo _____ con él. *(hablar)*
6. Tú nunca _____ con nosotros. *(comer)*

13. Complete the following sentences with the correct form of the pluperfect of the indicated verb.

1. Nosotros _____ a tiempo. *(llegar)*
2. Ellos _____ allí. *(comer)*
3. Tú _____ el viaje, ¿no? *(preparar)*
4. Ud. _____ a Ramírez, ¿no? *(conocer)*
5. Yo _____ antes. *(volver)*
6. El niño _____ el cristal. *(romper)*
7. ¿Quién te lo _____? *(decir)*
8. Nosotros nunca _____ tal cosa. *(hacer)*

14. Form sentences according to the model.

yo / comer / tener hambre
Yo habría comido pero no tenía hambre.

1. yo / terminar / tener tiempo
2. él / beber algo / tener sed
3. ellos / dormir / tener sueño
4. nosotros / ponernos una chaqueta / tener frío
5. yo / quitarme el suéter / tener calor
6. tú / hacer algo / tener miedo

The Subjunctive

The use of the subjunctive usually appears to be quite difficult for the speaker of English. The reason for this is that the subjunctive is seldom used in English, whereas it is widely used in Spanish. However, the use of the subjunctive is most logical once one understands the meaning of the word *subjunctive* as contrasted with the word *indicative*. Many grammar books categorize the types of verbs or expressions that must be followed by the subjunctive. Categories such as desire, sentiment, volition, cause, demand, request, doubt, necessity, etc., are given. This nearly endless list is quite difficult to remember when attempting to speak the language. The basic rule for knowing when to use the subjunctive is this: *Subjunctive implies subjectivity. If there exists the possibility that the action about which I am speaking has not or may not take place, it is necessary to use the subjunctive. However, if it is a realized fact that the action has taken or definitely will take place, the indicative is used.* Because of the indefinite nature of the subjunctive, it is almost always found in a dependent clause. It is introduced by some statement that lends subjectivity and vagueness to the definite realization of the action in the dependent clause. Study the following examples.

> *John is going to the store.*
> *John went to the store.*

In the two previous sentences, the speaker is relating an objective fact. Therefore the indicative is used.

> *I want John to go to the store.*
> *I tell John to go to the store.*
> *I hope John goes to the store.*
> *I prefer that John go to the store.*
> *It is necessary for John to go to the store.*
> *It is possible that John will go to the store.*

In all of the above statements, it is not fact that John will actually go to the store. For this reason all of these clauses would be in the subjunctive in Spanish. Whereas in English an infinitive construction is often used, in Spanish a clause must be used—*I want that John go to the store.* The only time a clause is not used is when there is no change of subject in the sentence.

> *I want to go to the store.*

To put it another way, if you have <u>two different subjects</u>—one in an independent clause and the second in a dependent clause—<u>and the action of the first subject influences or casts doubt on the action of the second subject</u>, then the verb that describes the second action is always in the subjunctive.

Note that the subjunctive may also be used in adverbial clauses.

> *I will see John as soon as he arrives.*
> *I will see John when he arrives.*

Since John has not yet arrived, the subjunctive would be used in the above sentences since there is no absolute guarantee that he will arrive.

> *I saw John as soon as he arrived.*
> *I saw John when he arrived.*

In the above sentences John has in reality arrived. For this reason, the indicative would be used.

Formation of the Present Subjunctive

Regular Verbs The root of the present subjunctive is the first person singular of the present indicative, without the ending **-o**. To this root, you add the subjunctive endings. The subjunctive endings are the reverse of those used for the indicative. The vowel **-e-** is used for **-ar** verbs and the vowel **-a-** is used for **-er** and **-ir** verbs.

hablar	comer	vivir
hable	coma	viva
hables	comas	vivas
hable	coma	viva
hablemos	comamos	vivamos
habléis	comáis	viváis
hablen	coman	vivan

Stem-changing Verbs Stem-changing verbs of the first class have the same change pattern as in the present indicative.

sentar	contar	perder	poder
siente	cuente	pierda	pueda
sientes	cuentes	pierdas	puedas
siente	cuente	pierda	pueda
sentemos	contemos	perdamos	podamos
sentéis	contéis	perdáis	podáis
sienten	cuenten	pierdan	puedan

Stem-changing verbs of the second class have an additional change in the first and second person plurals: an **-i-** or **-u-**.

preferir	dormir
prefiera	duerma
prefieras	duermas
prefiera	duerma
prefiramos	durmamos
prefiráis	durmáis
prefieran	duerman

Stem-changing verbs of the third class have the **-i-** in the stem of all forms of the present subjunctive.

pedir	seguir
pida	siga
pidas	sigas
pida	siga
pidamos	sigamos
pidáis	sigáis
pidan	sigan

Irregular Verbs

Infinitive	yo—Present indicative	Subjunctive
decir	digo	diga
hacer	hago	haga
oír	oigo	oiga
poner	pongo	ponga
tener	tengo	tenga
traer	traigo	traiga
salir	salgo	salga
valer	valgo	valga
venir	vengo	venga
conducir	conduzco	conduzca
conocer	conozco	conozca
traducir	traduzco	traduzca
construir	construyo	construya
influir	influyo	influya
caber	quepo	quepa

The common verbs **dar, ir, ser, estar,** and **saber** are irregular in the present subjunctive.

dar	ir	ser	estar	saber
dé	vaya	sea	esté	sepa
des	vayas	seas	estés	sepas
dé	vaya	sea	esté	sepa
demo	vayamos	seamos	estemos	sepamos
deis	vayáis	seáis	estéis	sepáis
den	vayan	sean	estén	sepan

Uses of the Present Subjunctive

In Noun Clauses As has already been explained, the subjunctive is required in clauses following verbs that denote a subjective idea or opinion. Such common verbs are:

querer	*to want*
esperar	*to hope*
estar contento	*to be happy*
sentir	*to regret*
temer	*to fear*
tener miedo de	*to be afraid*
preferir	*to prefer*
mandar	*to order*
insistir en	*to insist*
prohibir	*to prohibit*

In present-day speech it is common to hear also the future indicative after the verbs **esperar** and **temer.**

With Impersonal Expressions The subjunctive is also required after many impersonal expressions that denote subjectivity.

es bueno	*it is good*
es necesario	*it is necessary*
es preciso	*it is necessary*
es menester	*it is necessary*
es posible	*it is possible*
es imposible	*it is impossible*
es probable	*it is probable*
es malo	*it is bad*
es mejor	*it is better*
es lástima	*it is a pity*
es raro	*it is strange*
es importante	*it is important*
es fácil	*it is likely*
es difícil	*it is unlikely*
es aconsejable	*it is advisable*

conviene	*it is proper*
basta	*it is enough*
importa	*it is important*

Quiero que él venga y que me lo diga.
Prefiero que Uds. lo sepan.
Prohíben que salgamos.
Es necesario que él llegue temprano.
Es importante que Uds. lo hagan.

15. Complete the following with the correct subjunctive forms of the indicated verbs.
    1. Yo quiero que Uds. _____. *(hablar, comer, escribir, volver, dormir, seguir, venir, salir, conducir)*
    2. Ella prefiere que nosotros _____. *(terminar, prometer, empezar, servir, volver, salir, estar presentes, ir)*
    3. ¿Por qué mandas que yo _____? *(trabajar, leer, insistir, seguir, venir, dormir, salir, conducir, ir, ser así)*
    4. Él teme que tú no _____. *(estudiar, comer, volver, salir, dormir)*

16. Introduce the following sentences with the indicated expression.
    1. Nosotros recibimos los resultados. *(Es importante)*
    2. Ellos llegan por la mañana. *(Conviene que)*
    3. El chico estudia más. *(Es necesario)*
    4. Ellos vuelven pronto. *(Es posible)*
    5. El héroe pierde el juego. *(Es imposible)*
    6. Todos están presentes. *(Es mejor)*

With Expressions of Doubt When a statement of doubt introduces the main clause, the subjunctive appears in the dependent clause. The following are common expressions followed by the subjunctive.

no creer	*not to believe*
dudar	*to doubt*
es dudoso	*it is doubtful*
es incierto	*it is uncertain*
no es cierto	*it is not certain*
no estar seguro	*not to be sure*

If the introductory statement implies certainty, however, then the indicative (often in the future tense) appears in the dependent clause. The following are expressions followed by the indicative.

creer	*to believe*
no dudar	*not to doubt*
es cierto	*it is certain*
estar seguro	*to be sure*
no es dudoso	*it is not doubtful*
no hay duda	*there is no doubt*

No creo que ellos lleguen mañana.
Creo que ellos llegarán mañana.

With Special Verbs Verbs that imply a command, order, or advice also take the subjunctive, since it is not definite whether or not the order or advice will be carried out. The subject of the dependent clause is often indicated with an indirect object pronoun, even when the subject is named.

Le aconsejo a María que venga aquí.
I advise Mary to come here.

Juan le pide que lo ayude.
John asks her [him, you] to help him.

Note that with the verbs **decir** and **escribir** the subjunctive is used only when a command or an order is implied. When telling or writing someone about something, the indicative is used.

Yo le digo a Carlos que estudie.
I tell Charles to study.

Él me escribe que yo vuelva a casa.
He writes me to return home.

Carlos me dice que él no puede asistir.
Charles tells me that he cannot attend.

María me escribe que su padre está enfermo.
Mary writes me that her father is ill.

In Relative Clauses with Indefinite Antecedents The subjunctive appears in relative clauses when the antecedent (the word that the clause modifies) is indefinite. Note that the personal **a** is omitted when the object is indefinite.

> **Necesito un médico que hable español.**
> *I need a doctor who speaks Spanish.*
>
> **Conozco a un médico que habla español.**
> *I know a doctor who speaks Spanish.*

17. Complete the following sentences with the correct form of the indicated verb.

1. Es cierto que ellos _____ aquí mañana. *(estar)*
2. Dudo que tú lo _____ terminar. *(poder)*
3. No creo que Uds. lo _____. *(tener)*
4. No hay duda que nosotros _____. *(volver)*
5. Es dudoso que el profesor _____. *(asistir)*
6. Dudamos que ellos _____ tal viaje. *(hacer)*
7. Estoy seguro de que él _____. *(contestar)*
8. Es incierto que _____ hoy los resultados. *(llegar)*

18. Rewrite the following sentences with the correct form of the indicated verbs.

1. Yo le digo a Carlos que _____ más. *(trabajar, estudiar, comer, leer, escribir)*
2. Yo les aconsejo a ellos que no lo _____. *(comprar, vender, pedir, servir, hacer, traer, traducir)*
3. Mi madre me ruega que no _____. *(fumar, salir, ir, seguir, dormir)*
4. El señor nos sugiere que _____. *(esperar, trabajar, prometer, volver, salir, conducir)*

19. Complete the following sentences with the correct form of the indicated expressions.

1. Conozco a una secretaria que _____. *(hablar español, escribir bien, conocer la computadora)*
2. Necesito una secretaria que _____. *(hablar español, escribir bien, conocer la computadora)*

With superlatives The subjunctive is sometimes used in a relative clause that modifies a superlative expression. It suggests that the statement is merely an opinion.

Es el médico más inteligente que yo conozca.
He is the most intelligent doctor I know.

With negative expressions The subjunctive appears in a relative clause that modifies a negative word or expression.

No hay nadie que lo sepa.
There is nobody that knows it.

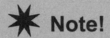

✳ Note!

After por... que

The subjunctive appears after adjectival and adverbial expressions introduced by **por... que** (*However . . .* , *No matter how . . .*) since they imply uncertainty.

Por atrevidos que sean, no van a ganar la batalla.
However daring they may be, they will not win the battle.

In Indefinite Expressions with *-quiera* Many words are made indefinite by attaching **-quiera** (*-ever*). Such words are followed by the subjunctive.

quienquiera	*whoever*
cuandoquiera	*whenever*
dondequiera	*wherever*
comoquiera	*however*
cualquiera	*whatever*

Quienquiera que sea, no te podrá ayudar.
Whoever [that] it may be, he will not be able to help you.

Dondequiera que vayas, no verás tal belleza.
Wherever you may go, you will not see such beauty.

The Imperfect Subjunctive

The imperfect subjunctive appears in clauses when the main clause is in a past tense or the conditional tense. The following diagram shows the usual sequence of tenses.

Main Clause	Dependent Clause
Present *Future* }	*Present Subjunctive*
Imperfect *Preterite* } *Conditional*	*Imperfect Subjunctive*

Él quiere que tú lo hagas.
Él querrá que tú lo hagas.

Él quería que tú lo hicieras.
Él querría que tú lo hicieras.

Formation of the Imperfect Subjunctive

The third person plural of the preterite serves as the root for the imperfect subjunctive. To this root are added the personal endings **-ara, -aras, -ara, -áramos, -arais, -aran** to **-ar** verbs and **-iera, -ieras, -iera, -iéramos, -ierais, -ieran** to **-er** and **-ir** verbs.

hablar	comer	vivir
hablara	comiera	viviera
hablaras	comieras	vivieras
hablara	comiera	viviera
habláramos	comiéramos	viviéramos
hablarais	comierais	vivierais
hablaran	comieran	vivieran

The imperfect subjunctive has a second set of endings. These endings are seldom used in conversation.

hablase	comiese	viviese
hablases	comieses	vivieses
hablase	comiese	viviese
hablásemos	comiésemos	viviésemos
hablaseis	comieseis	vivieseis
hablasen	comiesen	viviesen

The imperfect subjunctive of stem-changing and irregular verbs follows a regular pattern. The third person plural of the preterite serves as the root.

Infinitive	Preterite	Imperfect subjunctive
sentir	sintieron	sintiera
morir	murieron	muriera
pedir	pidieron	pidiera
andar	anduvieron	anduviera
estar	estuvieron	estuviera
tener	tuvieron	tuviera
poder	pudieron	pudiera
poner	pusieron	pusiera
saber	supieron	supiera
hacer	hicieron	hiciera
querer	quisieron	quisiera
venir	vinieron	viniera

Note that the following irregular verbs have the endings **-era** instead of **-iera** and **-eran** instead of **-ieran**.

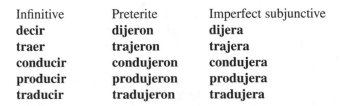

Infinitive	Preterite	Imperfect subjunctive
decir	dijeron	dijera
traer	trajeron	trajera
conducir	condujeron	condujera
producir	produjeron	produjera
traducir	tradujeron	tradujera

atribuir	atribuyeron	atribuyera
construir	construyeron	construyera
contribuir	contribuyeron	contribuyera
leer	leyeron	leyera
ir	fueron	fuera
ser	fueron	fuera

Uses of the Imperfect Subjunctive

In Noun Clauses The same noun clauses that require the present subjunctive require the imperfect subjunctive when the verb of the main clause is in the imperfect, preterite, or conditional.

> **Prefería que nosotros saliéramos.**
> **Prefirió que nosotros saliéramos.**
> **Preferiría que nosotros saliéramos.**

With Impersonal Expressions The imperfect subjunctive is used after impersonal expressions when the main verb is in the imperfect, preterite, or conditional.

> **Era necesario que tú estuvieras presente.**
> **Fue necesario que estuvieras presente.**
> **Sería necesario que estuvieras presente.**

In Relative Clauses Clauses that modify an indefinite antecedent when the verb of the main clause is in the imperfect, preterite, or conditional require the imperfect subjunctive.

> **Buscaban una secretaria que hablara español.**

20. Complete the following sentences with the correct form of the indicated verb.

1. Él insistió en que yo _____ en seguida. *(terminar)*
2. Ella prohibió que nosotros _____ café. *(beber)*
3. Ellos preferían que nosotros no _____. *(cantar)*
4. Él prefirió que tú _____ con una familia. *(vivir)*

5. Su padre insistió en que Juan _____. *(estudiar)*
6. Él me aconsejaría que yo _____ temprano. *(salir)*
7. El profesor no quería que nosotros _____ la poesía. *(traducir)*
8. Ella les escribió que _____ en seguida. *(volver)*
9. El profesor exigió que todos _____ a la reunión. *(ir)*
10. Él insistiría en que tú le _____ en español. *(hablar)*

21. Rewrite the following sentences changing the main verb to the imperfect.

1. Insisten en que comamos con ellos.
2. Tienen miedo de que no vuelvas.
3. Ella prefiere que vengas a las ocho.
4. Quieren que hagamos el viaje en tren.
5. Insiste en que tú lo repitas.
6. Temen que no lo sepamos.

The Subjunctive with Adverbial Conjunctions

Conjunctions of Time The subjunctive appears after adverbial conjunctions of time when the verb of the main clause is in the future, since you cannot be certain that the action in the adverbial clause will take place. When the verb is in the past, however, the indicative and not the subjunctive is used, since the action has already been realized.

> **Yo le hablaré cuando venga.**
> *I will speak to him when he comes.*

> **Yo le hablé cuando vino.**
> *I spoke to him when he came.*

The following are common adverbial conjunctions of time.

cuando	*when*
en cuanto	*as soon as*
tan pronto como	*as soon as*
luego que	*as soon as*
hasta que	*until*
después de que	*after*

Remember

The conjunction **antes de que** *(before)* always takes the subjunctive.

Ellos saldrán antes de que lleguemos.
They will leave before we arrive.

Ellos salieron antes de que llegáramos.
They left before we arrived.

With *aunque (although)* The speaker determines whether or not to use the subjunctive after **aunque**. Study the following examples.

> **Él saldrá aunque llueva.**
> *(He will go out even though it may rain. It isn't raining now.)*
>
> **Él saldrá aunque llueve.**
> *(He will go out even though it's raining—and it is now.)*

Other Conjunctions Following is a list of other conjunctions that also take the subjunctive.

sin que	*without*
con tal de que	*provided that*
en caso de que	*in case*
a menos que	*unless*
a pesar de que	*in spite of*

> **Él saldrá sin que ellos lo sepan.**
> **Él salió sin que ellos lo supieran.**
>
> **Yo no haré el viaje a menos que lo hagas tú.**
> **Yo no haría el viaje a menos que lo hicieras tú.**

Conjunctions of Purpose The following conjunctions of purpose normally take the subjunctive.

de manera que	so that
de modo que	so that
para que	in order that
a fin de que	in order that

Él lo hará de manera que nos sea fácil.
Él lo haría de manera que nos fuera fácil.

Ella habla así para que comprendamos.
Ella habló así para que comprendiéramos.

Note that in very special cases when the speaker is sure that the desired result was realized, the indicative can be used.

**El capitán quemó el barco de modo que no pudo subir
el enemigo.**
*The captain burnt the ship so that the enemy
could not board. (And the enemy didn't.)*

Quizá, Tal vez, Ojalá The expressions **quizá, tal vez** *(perhaps)*, and **ojalá** *(would that)* can be followed by either the present or imperfect subjunctive.

¡Quizá esté presente!	*Perhaps he is present.*
¡Tal vez estuviera presente!	*Perhaps he was present.*
¡Ojalá vengan ellos!	*I hope they come!*
¡Ojalá vinieran ellos!	*If only they would come!*

You Need to Know ✓

Quisiera

The imperfect subjunctive of **querer** is commonly used in independent clauses. It is a more polite form than **quiero** *(I want)*, etc., and is equivalent to *I would like*.

Quisiera un vaso de agua.
I'd like a glass of water.

22. Complete the following sentences with the correct form of the indicated verbs.
    1. Ellos saldrán cn cuanto nosotros _____. *(hablar, comenzar, comer, salir, llegar, servir)*
    2. Ellos salieron en cuanto nosotros _____. *(hablar, comenzar, comer, salir, llegar, servir)*
    3. Yo esperaré hasta que Uds. _____. *(terminar, cantar, comer, salir, llegar, volver)*
    4. Yo esperé hasta que Uds. _____. *(terminar, cantar, comer, salir, llegar, volver)*
    5. Ella hablará antes de que yo _____. *(hablar, terminar, volver, salir)*
    6. Ella habló antes de que yo _____. *(hablar, entrar, terminar, volver, salir)*

23. Complete the following sentences with the correct form of the indicated verb according to the idea conveyed in parentheses.
    1. Ellos vendrán aunque no _____. *(estar)* (No saben si voy a estar.)
    2. Voy al centro aunque _____. *(llover)* (Está lloviendo ahora.)
    3. No voy a terminar aunque _____ todo el día. *(trabajar)* (No sé si voy a trabajar tanto.)
    4. Él no lo comprará aunque _____ rico. *(ser)* (No sé si es rico.)

24. Complete the following sentences with the correct form of the indicated verb.
    1. Yo podré hacerlo sin que ellos me _____. *(ayudar)*
    2. No podríamos hacerlo sin que tú nos _____. *(ayudar)*
    3. En caso de que ellos no _____ a tiempo, no podré esperar. *(llegar)*
    4. Yo iría con tal de que _____ Uds. *(ir)*
    5. Yo iré con tal de que _____ Uds. *(ir)*

Present Perfect Subjunctive

The present perfect subjunctive is formed by using the present subjunctive of the auxiliary verb **haber** and the past participle.

hablar	comer	vivir
haya hablado	haya comido	haya vivido
hayas hablado	hayas comido	hayas vivido
haya hablado	haya comido	haya vivido
hayamos hablado	hayamos comido	hayamos vivido
hayáis hablado	hayáis comido	hayáis vivido
hayan hablado	hayan comido	hayan vivido

It is necessary to use the present perfect subjunctive when a present or future verb in a main clause governs a verb which refers to a past action.

No creo que ellos hayan llegado.
I don't believe they have arrived.

No creerá que tú hayas llegado.
He won't believe that you have arrived.

Pluperfect Subjunctive

The pluperfect subjunctive is formed by using the imperfect subjunctive of the auxiliary verb **haber** and the past participle.

hablar	comer	vivir
hubiera hablado	hubiera comido	hubiera vivido
hubieras hablado	hubieras comido	hubieras vivido
hubiera hablado	hubiera comido	hubiera vivido
hubiéramos hablado	hubiéramos comido	hubiéramos vivido
hubierais hablado	hubierais comido	hubierais vivido
hubieran hablado	hubieran comido	hubieran vivido

The pluperfect subjunctive appears in clauses following a verb in a past tense, when the action of the verb of the dependent clause was completed prior to that of the governing verb.

Él quería que hubiéramos llegado antes.
He wanted us to have arrived before.

Él habría preferido que tú lo hubieras sabido antes.
He would have preferred that you had known it before.

Él no creyó que ellos hubieran hecho tal cosa.
He didn't believe that they had [would have] done such a
*   thing.*

Si **clauses** Si clauses express contrary-to-fact conditions. The sequence
of tenses is as follows.

Main clause	Si clause
Future	*Present Indicative*
Conditional	*Imperfect Subjunctive*
Conditional Perfect	*Pluperfect Subjunctive*

Haré el viaje si tengo el dinero.
I will take the trip if I have the money.

Haría el viaje si tuviera el dinero.
I would take the trip if I had the money.

Habría hecho el viaje si hubiera tenido el dinero
I would have taken the trip if I had had the money.

Remember

The present subjunctive never appears
after **si**.

Many speakers of Spanish substitute the pluperfect subjunctive for the
conditional perfect in the main clause.

Hubiéramos hecho el viaje si hubiéramos tenido el dinero.
We would have made the trip if we had had the money.

25. Complete the following sentences with the correct form of the present perfect subjunctive of the indicated verb.

1. Ella está contenta de que tú _____. *(llegar)*
2. Él tiene miedo de que nosotros les _____ todo. *(decir)*
3. Es posible que ellos no te _____. *(conocer)*
4. No creo que él _____. *(terminar)*
5. Es una lástima que Uds. _____ tanto. *(sufrir)*
6. Espero que Ud. lo _____ bien. *(pasar)*

26. Complete the following sentences with the correct form of the pluperfect subjunctive of the indicated verb.

1. Fue imposible que aquel niño _____ tanto. *(comer)*
2. Era probable que ellos lo _____ antes. *(saber)*
3. Carlos quería que nosotros lo _____ antes de su llegada. *(discutir)*
4. Perferíamos esperar hasta que ellos _____. *(salir)*
5. Él temía que tú no _____. *(terminar)*

27. Complete the following sentences with the correct form of the indicated verb according to the regular sequence of tenses.

1. Ellos irán si _____ bastante tiempo. *(tener)*
2. Yo saldré si no _____. *(llover)*
3. Yo iré de compras si tú me _____. *(acompañar)*
4. Él trabajaría más si no _____ tan cansado. *(estar)*
5. Nosotros pagaríamos ahora si _____ ir al banco. *(poder)*
6. ¿No irías tú a España si _____ billete? *(tener)*
7. Él me lo habría dicho si lo _____. *(saber)*
8. Habrían llegado a la hora indicada si el avión _____ a tiempo. *(salir)*

The Imperative

Formal Commands The formal command (**Ud.** and **Uds.**) commands are the same as the **Ud.** and **Uds.** present subjunctive forms. *(Refer to page 57.)*

> **Hable usted más alto.**
> **¡Vengan! ¡Pasen Uds.!**

Familiar Commands The familiar **tú** affirmative command has the same form as the third person singular (**Ud.**) indicative form of the verb. The pronoun **tú** is usually omitted.

cantar	canta
aprender	aprende
escribir	escribe
pensar	piensa
volver	vuelve
dormir	duerme
pedir	pide
servir	sirve

The following verbs have irregular forms for the familiar command.

tener	ten
poner	pon
venir	ven
salir	sal
hacer	haz
decir	di
ser	sé
ir	ve

Familiar negative **tú** commands are the same as the **tú** form of the present subjunctive.

hablar	no hables
comer	no comas
escribir	no escribas

The familiar plural command (**Uds.**) is the same as the formal command since in most Spanish-speaking countries there is no differentiation between the formal and familiar forms in the plural. In Spain, however, the **vosotros** form of the command is used. The **vosotros** form of the command is formed by dropping the **-r** of the infinitive and replacing it with **-d.**

	Spain	*Other areas*
hablar	hablad	hablen Uds.
comer	comed	coman Uds.
recibir	recibid	reciban Uds.
pensar	pensad	piensen Uds.
pedir	pedid	pidan Uds.
salir	salid	salgan Uds.
hacer	haced	hagan Uds.

First Person Plural Command (Let's) This command is the same as the first person plural of the present subjunctive.

Comamos allí.	*Let's eat there.*
Salgamos pronto.	*Let's leave soon.*

The only exception is the verb **ir.**

Vamos ahora.	*Let's go now.*

With *ir a* The idea of *Let's* can also be expressed by using **vamos a** with the infinitive.

Vamos a cantar.	*Let's sing.*
Vamos a comer.	*Let's eat.*
Vamos a salir.	*Let's leave.*

28. Complete the following sentences with the correct singular formal form of the command of the indicated verb.

1. _____ la Avenida de San Martín. *(tomar)*
2. _____ derecho hasta el final. *(seguir)*
3. _____ a la derecha. *(doblar)*
4. _____ a la tercera bocacalle. *(ir)*
5. _____ la autopista. La verá Ud. a mano derecha. *(tomar)*
6. _____ hasta la primera garita de peaje. *(seguir)*
7. _____ el peaje. *(pagar)*
8. _____ hasta la segunda salida. *(seguir)*
9. _____ en la segunda salida después de pagar el peaje. *(salir)*
10. _____ a la derecha. *(virar)*
11. _____ los rótulos hasta llegar a Monterrey. *(seguir)*
12. ¡Y_____ muy buen viaje! *(tener)*

29. Answer the following questions with the familiar command according to the model.

¿Hablo?
Sí, habla.

1. ¿Nado?
2. ¿Canto?
3. ¿Bailo?
4. ¿Trabajo?
5. ¿Leo?
6. ¿Como?
7. ¿Escribo la carta?

30. Answer the following questions with the familiar command according to the model.

¿Tener prisa?
Ten prisa.

1. ¿Tener suerte?
2. ¿Tener tiempo?
3. ¿Poner todo en orden?
4. ¿Poner la mesa?
5. ¿Venir en seguida?
6. ¿Venir mañana?
7. ¿Salir ahora?
8. ¿Salir de noche?

31. Rewrite the following commands in the negative of the **tú** form.

1. Habla.	7. Vuelve.
2. Nada.	8. Pide.
3. Come.	9. Sirve.
4. Bebe.	10. Ven.
5. Escribe.	11. Sal más.
6. Piensa.	12. Ten más paciencia.

The Present Participle

The present participle of **-ar** verbs consists of the verb root plus **-ando**.
The present participle **-er** and **-ir** verbs consists of the root plus **-iendo**.

hablar	**hablando**	*speaking*
comer	**comiendo**	*eating*
salir	**saliendo**	*leaving*

Many stem-changing **-ir** verbs also have a stem change in the present participle.

sentir	**sintiendo**
dormir	**durmiendo**

Verbs such as **construir, oír,** and **leer**, which have a **-y-** in the preterite also have the **-y-** in the present participle.

construir	**construyendo**
oír	**oyendo**
leer	**leyendo**

The verb **ir** is irregular.

ir	**yendo**

The present participle is seldom used alone. It is sometimes used, however, to express an entire clause.

Construyendo el puente, se cayó.
While he was constructing the bridge, he fell.

Yendo al mercado, vio a su amiga.
[As he was] going to the market, he saw his friend.

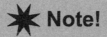

Note!

Present participle

The most common use of the present participle is with the progressive tenses. A description of these tenses follows.

Progressive Tenses

The progressive tenses show that the action of the verb is taking place. The most commonly used tenses are the present and the imperfect. The progressive tense combines the appropriate tense of **estar** (also **seguir, ir, andar**) with the present participle.

Present Progressive

hablar	comer	salir
estoy hablando	estoy comiendo	estoy saliendo
estás hablando	estás comiendo	estás saliendo
está hablando	está comiendo	está saliendo
estamos hablando	estamos comiendo	estamos saliendo
estáis hablando	estáis comiendo	estáis saliendo
están hablando	están comiendo	están saliendo

Imperfect Progressive

comer	beber	pedir
estaba nadando	estaba bebiendo	estaba pidiendo
estabas nadando	estabas bebiendo	estabas pidiendo
estaba nadando	estaba bebiendo	estaba pidiendo
estábamos nadando	estábamos bebiendo	estábamos pidiendo
estabais nadando	estabais bebiendo	estabais pidiendo
estaban nadando	estaban bebiendo	estaban pidiendo

Ellos están nadando en el mar.
They are swimming in the sea. (right now)

El niño va comiendo un sandwich.
The child goes along eating a sandwich. (right now)

Ellos seguían trabajando.
They kept on working.

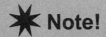

Note!

The progressive forms are never used with **ir** and **venir**.

Iba al parque. *He was going to the park.*

---

32. Rewrite the following sentences using the present progressive.

1. María canta y Juan toca la guitarra.
2. Las chicas preparan la lección.
3. Yo pongo la mesa.
4. Comemos en el restaurante.
5. El avión sale.
6. Ellos viven con nosotros.

33. Rewrite the following sentences using the imperfect progressive.

1. Él charlaba con sus amigos.
2. Ellos hacían un viaje por España.
3. Aquellos señores trabajaban como bestias.
4. Yo no comía nada.
5. Él salía con María.
6. El profesor explicaba la teoría.
7. Construíamos una carretera en el interior.
8. Ella no pedía nada.

Reflexive Verbs

Formation A reflexive verb is one in which the action is both executed and received by the subject. Since the subject also receives the action, an additional pronoun is needed. This is called the reflexive pronoun.

lavarse *(to wash)*	**levantarse** *(to get up)*
me lavo	me levanto
te lavas	te levantas
se lava	se levanta
nos lavamos	nos levantamos
os laváis	os levantáis
se lavan	se levantan

Other common regular reflexive verbs are:

cepillarse	*to brush oneself*
ducharse	*to take a shower*
peinarse	*to comb one's hair*
marcharse	*to leave, go away*
quitarse	*to take off clothing*

Common stem-changing reflexive verbs are:

acostarse (ue)	*to go to bed*
despertarse (ie)	*to wake up*
sentarse (ie)	*to sit down*
despedirse de (i, i)	*to take leave*
dormirse (ue, u)	*to fall asleep*
vestirse (i, i)	*to dress oneself*

A common irregular verb that is used reflexively is **ponerse** *(to put on clothing)*.

acostarse	**vestirse**	**ponerse**
me acuesto	me visto	me pongo
te acuestas	te vistes	te pones
se acuesta	se viste	se pone

nos acostamos	nos vestimos	nos ponemos
os acostáis	os vestís	os ponéis
se acuestan	se visten	se ponen

Special Note Concerning Reflexive Verbs The following verbs can be used with or without the reflexive pronoun.

bajar	bajarse	*to get off*
desembarcar	desembarcarse	*to disembark*
embarcar	embarcarse	*to embark*
enfermar	enfermarse	*to get sick*
parar	pararse	*to stop*
pasear	pasearse	*to stroll*
subir	subirse	*to get on*

The reflexive pronoun is more commonly used in Latin America than in Spain.

You will note that with parts of the body and articles of clothing, the possessive adjectives are omitted when used with a reflexive verb. Study the following differences between Spanish and English.

Me lavé la cara.	*I washed my face.*
Juan se quita la chaqueta.	*John takes off his jacket.*

You will also note that even though the noun is ordinarily pluralized in English, it is in the singular in Spanish.

Ellos se lavan la cara.	*They wash their faces.*
Ellos se quitan el sombrero.	*They take off their hats.*

Reflexive versus Nonreflexive Many verbs can be used both reflexively and nonreflexively. Note that the reflexive pronoun is used only when the action refers to the subject.

Juan se lava.	*John washes himself.*
Juan lava el carro.	*John washes the car.*

El padre se acuesta.	*The father goes to bed.*
El padre acuesta al niño.	*The father puts the child to bed.*

Reciprocal Verbs A reciprocal verb is one in which people do something to or for each other. In Spanish a reciprocal verb functions exactly the same as a reflexive verb. Study the following examples.

> **Ellos se vieron y se reconocieron en seguida.**
> *They saw each another and they recognized each
> other immediately.*

> **Los dos hermanos se parecen mucho.**
> *The two brothers look alike (look a lot like each other).*

> **Nos escribimos muy a menudo.**
> *We write to one another often.*

34. Complete the following sentences with the correct reflexive pronoun.

1. Yo _____ acuesto a las once.
2. Juan _____ afeita cada mañana.
3. María _____ quita el suéter.
4. Nosotros _____ cepillamos los dientes.
5. ¿Por qué no _____ peinas?
6. Ellos _____ sientan a nuestra mesa.

35. Complete the following sentences with the correct form of the present tense of the indicated verb.

1. Yo siempre _____ temprano. *(acostarse)*
2. Ella _____ cada mañana. *(bañarse)*
3. Nosotros _____ los dientes. *(cepillarse)*
4. La niña _____ en el espejo y _____.
   (mirarse, peinarse)
5. ¿Por qué no _____ tú con nosotros? *(sentarse)*

36. Complete the following sentences with the correct definite article or possessive adjective.

1. El niño se lava _____ cara.
2. Yo me pongo _____ corbata.
3. No sé dónde está _____ corbata.
4. Los señores se quitaron _____ sombrero.

    5. María, _____ falda es muy bonita.

    6. Él se cepilla _____ dientes.

37. Complete the following sentences with the correct reflexive pronoun when necessary.

    1. Juan _____ pone la chaqueta.

    2. Juan _____ la chaqueta en el baúl.

    3. Ellos _____ lavan los platos.

    4. Ellos _____ lavan las manos.

    5. Nosotros _____ acostamos al bebé.

    6. Nosotros _____ acostamos tarde.

    7. Yo _____ visto en seguida.

    8. Yo _____ visto primero y luego _____ visto a las niñas.

Special Uses of the Infinitive

After a Preposition The infinitive is always used after a preposition in Spanish, whereas in English the present participle is used.

> **Yo le hablé antes de salir.**
> *I spoke to him before leaving.*

The word **al** with the infinitive means *upon, when, as.*

> **Al salir, me despedí de mis amigos.**
> *Upon leaving, I took leave of [said good-bye to] my friends.*

As a Noun The infinitive either alone or accompanied by the definite article **el** can function as a noun. English uses the present participle more often than the infinitive as the verbal noun.

> **No puedo aguantar el fumar.**
> *I can't stand smoking.*

> **Leer sin luz suficiente puede perjudicar los ojos.**
> *Reading without sufficient light can harm your eyes.*

Passive Voice

With *ser* The passive voice is less commonly used in Spanish than in English. Spanish speakers prefer to use the active voice. When the true passive voice is used, however, it is formed by using the verb **ser** plus the past participle. The agent or person who performed the action is introduced by **por**. **Por** is replaced by **de** if emotion is involved. Note that the past participle agrees with the subject.

Las cartas fueron entregadas por el cartero
The letters were delivered by the letter carrier.

Aquel soldado fue admirado de todos.
That soldier was admired by all.

The most common usage of the passive voice is an abbreviated form of the passive used for newspaper headlines.

**Niño de ocho años atropellado
por automóvil.**
Eight-year-old boy hit by car.

Pueblo destruido por terremoto.
Town destroyed by earthquake.

With *se* A common way to form the passive voice is by using the reflexive pronoun **se** with the third person singular or plural of the verb. This construction is most common when the person by whom the action is carried out (agent) is unimportant.

Se venden corbatas en aquella tienda.
Neckties are sold in that store.

Se ve el mejor monumento en el centro del pueblo.
The best monument is seen in the center of town.

This construction is also used to convey an indefinite subject.

Se dice que él está enfermo.
They say that he is ill. (It is said that he is ill.)

Se oye que la situación es mejor.
One hears that the situation is better. (It is heard that the situation is better.)

38. Complete the following sentences.
1. El dinero _____ robado _____ el ladrón.
2. La muela _____ sacada _____ el dentista.
3. La casa _____ destruida _____ el incendio.
4. Las tropas _____ derrotadas _____ las fuerzas enemigas.

39. Complete the following sentences.
1. ¿A qué hora _____ la tienda. *(cerrarse)*
2. ¿Cómo _____ *apple* en español? *(decirse)*
3. _____ madera para construir una casa. *(usarse)*
4. Desde allí _____ los volcanes. *(verse)*
5. _____ coches en aquella fábrica. *(hacerse)*
6. ¿Cuándo _____ el museo? *(abrirse)*

Chapter 4
PRONOUNS

IN THIS CHAPTER:

✔ *Subject Pronouns*
✔ *Object Pronouns*
✔ *Reflexive Pronouns*
✔ *Prepositional Pronouns*
✔ *Possessive Pronouns*
✔ *Demonstrative Pronouns*
✔ *Relative Pronouns*

Subject Pronouns

The subject pronouns in Spanish are:

yo	*I*	**nosotros(as)**	*we*
tú	*you*	**vosotros(as)**	*you*
él	*he, it*	**ellos**	*they*
ella	*she, it*	**ellas**	*they*
usted	*you*	**ustedes**	*you*

There are four standard ways to say *you*. The pronoun **tú** is for familiar

87

and informal address, with relations, friends, children, and animals. In Spain, **vosotros(as)** is the plural form of **tú.** In most of Spanish America **ustedes** is the plural of **tú.**

In Argentina, Uruguay, Paraguay, and a few other areas, you will hear the familiar singular pronoun **vos,** used with verbs similar to the **vosotros** forms, instead of **tú.**

Usted, ustedes are formal forms of address, for persons whom you do not know well, to whom you wish to show respect, or for persons older than yourself. **Usted** is a contraction of **vuestra merced,** *your grace.* Like "Your Honor" in old English, it is used with the third person. It is often abbreviated, with a capital letter, **Ud., Uds.** (or **Vd., Vds.,** in older texts).

¿Cómo está Ud.?	*How are you?*
¿Cómo están Uds.?	*How are you [all]?*

You Need to Know ✓

Since the verb ending in Spanish indicates what the subject of the verb is, it is common to omit the subject pronouns, especially **yo, tú, nosotros(as), vosotros(as).**

Hablas español con el profesor.
You speak Spanish with the teacher.

The subject pronouns are used after the comparative construction.

Él tiene más años que yo.
He is older than I.

Ella tiene tanto dinero como tú.
She has as much money as you.

1. Complete the following with the correct subject pronouns.

    1. _____ tenemos que salir en seguida.

    2. _____ llegas muy tarde.

    3. _____ no queremos discutirlo.

    4. _____ estoy muy bien.

    5. ¿_____ preparas la fiesta?

    6. ¿Cómo está _____, señora Romero?

    7. _____ lo traigo en seguida.

2. Complete the following sentences.

    1. Ella tiene más paciencia que _____. *(I)*

    2. Ellos viajan con más frecuencia que _____. *(we)*

    3. Carlos no lee tanto como _____. *(you)*

    4. Ella trabaja más horas que _____. *(he)*

Object Pronouns

Direct Object Pronouns The direct object pronouns **lo, la, los,** and **las** can refer to either persons or things. They precede the conjugated form of the verb.

María saluda a Juan.	**María lo saluda.**
Mary greets John.	*Mary greets him.*
Juan lee el libro.	**Juan lo lee.**
John reads the book.	*John reads it.*
Conocemos a las hijas de Carlos.	**Las conocemos bien.**
We know Charles's daughters.	*We know them well.*
Carlos tiene las fotografías.	**Carlos las tiene.**
Charles has the tickets.	*Charles has them.*

Direct and Indirect Object Pronouns *Me Te Nos* The pronouns **me, te,** and **nos** can function as either direct objects or indirect objects.

Carlos me ve.	**Carlos me habla.**
Charles sees me.	*Charles speaks to me.*

Ella no te conoce.	**Ella no te dice nada.**
She doesn't know you.	*She doesn't tell you anything.*
El niño nos mira.	**El niño nos da sus juguetes.**
The child looks at us.	*The child gives us his toys.*

The direct and indirect object pronoun that corresponds to the subject **vosotros** is **os.**

El soldado os ve.	**El soldado os habla.**
The soldier sees you.	*The soldier is talking to you.*

Indirect Object Pronouns *Le, Les* The third person indirect object pronoun is **le** in the singular and **les** in the plural for both masculine and feminine. To identify the indirect object clearly, a prepositional phrase often accompanies **le** and **les.**

Yo le hablo a él.
Yo le hablo a ella.
Yo le hablo a Ud.

Él les da los informes a ellos.
Él les da los informes a ellas.
Él les da los informes a Uds.

The pronouns **le** and **les** are commonly used even if there is a noun object in the sentence.

Le di la carta a María.
Él les mandó los informes a sus amigos.

Double Object Pronouns *Me lo, Te lo, Nos lo* In many cases, both a direct and indirect object pronoun will appear in the same sentence. When such occurs, the indirect object pronoun always precedes the direct object pronoun.

Juan me lo dijo.	*John told it to me.*
María nos los enseñó.	*Mary showed them to us.*
Juan te lo explicó.	*John explained it to you.*

Se lo The indirect object pronouns **le** and **les** both change to **se** when used with the direct object pronouns **lo, la, los, las**. Since the pronoun **se** can have many meanings, it is often clarified by the use of a prepositional phrase.

> **Él se lo dice a él (a ella, a Ud., a ellos, a ellas, a Uds.).**
> *He tells it to him (to her, to you, to them, to them, to you).*

> **Ellos se lo explican a él (a ella, a Ud., a ellos, a ellas, a Uds.).**
> *They explain it to him (to her, to you, to them, to them, to you).*

3. Complete the following sentences with the correct pronoun.

1. Tomás mira a su hija. Tomás _____ mira.
2. Juan tiene las fotografías. Juan _____ tiene.
3. El padre acostó al niño. El padre _____ acostó.
4. Ellas discutieron el problema. Ellas _____ discutieron.
5. Él perdió la novela. Él _____ perdió.
6. Tenemos los billetes. _____ tenemos.

4. Complete the following mini-conversation with the correct pronouns.

—¿_____ llamó Pepe?
—Sí, él _____ llamó.
—¿Qué _____ dijo?
—_____ dijo todo lo que había pasado. Lo siento pero no _____ voy a decir nada.

5. Rewrite the following sentences, substituting the italicized indirect object with a pronoun.

1. Él dijo la verdad *a María*.
2. El cartero dio las cartas *a Juan*.
3. El señor González habló *a sus hijos*.
4. Yo di un regalo *a mi hermana*.

6. Answer the following questions according to the model.

¿Quién te compró la blusa?
Mamá me la compró.

1. ¿Quién te compró los zapatos?
2. ¿Quién te compró la pollera?
3. ¿Quién te compró las medias?
4. ¿Quién te compró los jeans?

7. Rewrite the following sentences, substituting pronouns for the direct and indirect objects.

1. Carlos le dio las recetas a su amiga.
2. Yo le mandé el regalo a Carlos.
3. El profesor les explicó la lección a los alumnos.
4. La madre compró el abrigo para María.
5. El pasajero le dio los billetes al empleado.
6. María les leyó el cuento a las niñas.

Position of Object Pronouns with Conjugated Verbs The object pronouns always precede the conjugated form of the verb. If a sentence is negative, the negative word precedes the object pronouns. With compound tenses the object pronouns precede the auxiliary verb.

El profesor nos explicó la lección.
Él no me lo dijo.
Ellos te lo han dado.

With Infinitives The object pronouns can either be attached to the infinitive or precede the auxiliary verb. When two pronouns are attached to the infinitive, the infinitive carries a written accent mark to maintain the same stress.

Él me lo quiere explicar.	**Él quiere explicármelo.**
María te va a ayudar.	**María va a ayudarte.**

With Present Participles The pronouns can either precede the auxiliary verb **estar (seguir, andar)** or be attached to the present participle. The participle then requires a written accent mark to maintain the same stress.

Él está construyendo el puente.
Él lo está construyendo.
Él está construyéndolo.

8. Rewrite the following sentences according to the model.

Ella quiere mandar el telegrama a Teresa.
Ella se lo quiere mandar.
Ella quiere mandárselo.

1. Ella quiere darte el regalo.
2. Queremos devolver el libro al profesor.
3. Van a servir la comida al convidado.
4. El presidente prefiere dar la conferencia.
5. Ellos piensan vender el carro.

9. Rewrite the following sentences according to the model.

Ella siguió preparando la tarea.
Ella la siguió preparando.
Ella siguió preparándola.

1. Están cantándote la canción.
2. Está dedicando el libro al general.
3. Estamos sirviendo la comida a los clientes.
4. Ella está mostrándome las fotografías.
5. Él está preparándote el desayuno.

With Commands The object pronouns are always attached to the affirmative commands and always precede the negative commands. When necessary to maintain the stress, a written accent mark must appear.

Hágamelo Ud.	**No me lo haga Ud.**
Házmelo.	**No me lo hagas.**
Hágalo Ud.	**No lo haga Ud.**
Hazlo.	**No lo hagas.**

First person plural (Let's) The pronoun is attached in affirmative expressions with *let's*. It precedes the verb when the sentence is negative.

Ayudémoslo.	*Let's help him.*
No lo ayudemos.	*Let's not help him.*
Hagámoslo.	*Let's do it.*
No lo hagamos.	*Let's not do it.*

In the case of reflexive verbs, the final **-s** of the verb is dropped before the pronoun **nos**.

Sentémonos.
Let's sit down.

Levantémonos.
Let's get up.

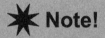

✳ Note!

Note the form of the verb **irse**.

Vámonos.   *Let's go. (Let's get going.)*

10. Rewrite the following sentences, substituting the objects with pronouns.

1. Suba Ud. las maletas.
2. Dígame Ud. el episodio.
3. Pida Ud. la ayuda.
4. Laven Uds. los platos.
5. Busca al perro.
6. Prepárame la comida.
7. Vende los carros.
8. No lea Ud. el libro.
9. No sirvan Uds. los refrescos.
10. No saque Ud. la fotografía.
11. No pongas la comida en la mesa.
12. No dé Ud. el dinero a Carlos.

11. Follow the model.

¿Acostarnos?
Sí, acostémonos.
No, no nos acostemos.

1. ¿Levantarnos?
2. ¿Lavarnos la cara?
3. ¿Prepararnos?
4. ¿Quitarnos la corbata?

Special Verbs with Indirect Objects Verbs such as **asustar** *(to scare),* **encantar** *(to enchant),* **enfurecer** *(to make one furious),* **enojar** *(to annoy),* and **sorprender** *(to surprise)* function the same in Spanish as in English. They are always used with the indirect object. In Spanish, the subject of the sentence often comes at the end.

Aquel ruido me asusta. / Me asusta aquel ruido.
¿Te encantan los bailes chilenos?
A Juan le enfurecen mis opiniones.
Nos enojan aquellos rumores.
Les sorprendió la noticia.

In Spanish there are two other verbs, **gustar** and **faltar (hacer falta),** that function in the same way. The verb **gustar** is translated into English as *to like* and **faltar** as *to need.* These verbs actually mean, however, *to be pleasing to* and *to be lacking.* For this reason, the English subject becomes an indirect object in Spanish.

Me gusta la comida.	*I like the meal.*
Me gustan los mariscos.	*I like shellfish.*
A Juan le gusta bailar.	*John likes to dance.*
A Juan le gustan los bailes.	*John likes the dances.*
Nos gusta la música.	*We like music.*
Nos gustan las canciones.	*We like the songs.*
Les gusta la idea.	*They like the idea.*
Les gustan los resultados.	*They like the results.*

12. Complete the following sentences with the correct indirect object pronoun and verb ending.

1. A mí _____ enfurec_____ aquella mosca.
2. A mí _____ sorprend_____ aquellas noticias.
3. A nosotros _____ encant_____ su programa de televisión.
4. A nosotros _____ enoj_____ sus opiniones.
5. A ti _____ asust_____ los ruidos, ¿no?

13. Rewrite the following sentences according to the model.

A mí / la langosta
Me gusta la langosta.

1. A nosotros / la música
2. A Pablo / las lenguas
3. A ellos / el proyecto
4. A ti / los programas
5. A Elena / el arte moderno

Reflexive Pronouns

The reflexive pronouns are used when the subject of the verb performs the action on itself. The reflexive pronouns are:

me	**nos**
te	**os**
se	**se**

For a review of reflexive verbs see pages 81–84.

Reflexive Pronouns with an Indirect Object Pronoun To express an involuntary or unexpected action, Spanish uses a reflexive pronoun with the indirect object pronoun. These expressions have no exact equivalent in English. The indirect object tells who is affected by the action.

Se me cayó el vaso.
I dropped the glass. (not on purpose, it fell out of my hand)

A Juan se le olvidaron los billetes.
John inadvertently forgot the tickets.

Prepositional Pronouns

Pronouns that follow a preposition are the same as the subject pronouns with the exception of **yo** and **tú**, which change to **mí** and **ti** after a preposition.

Subject	Prepositional	Subject	Prepositional
yo	mí	nosotros(as)	nosotros(as)
tú	ti	vosotros(as)	vosotros(as)
él	él	ellos	ellos
ella	ella	ellas	ellas
Ud.	Ud.	Uds.	Uds.

There is an accent on **mí** but not on **ti**, to distinguish the pronoun **mí** from the possessive adjective **mi**.

> **Están hablando de ti.**
> **No están hablando de mí.**
> **Ellos viven cerca de nosotros.**
> **Carlos quiere hablar con ella.**

With the preposition **con** *(with)*, the pronouns **mí** and **ti** are contracted to form one word.

> **Juan quiere ir conmigo.**
> **Yo quiero ir contigo.**

Possessive Pronouns

A possessive pronoun replaces a noun modified by a possessive adjective. It agrees with the noun that it replaces and is accompanied by the appropriate definite article.

Possessive Adjectives

mi, mis	**nuestro, nuestra, nuestros, nuestras**
tu, tus	**vuestro, vuestra, vuestros, vuestras**
su, sus	**su, sus**

Possessive Pronouns
el mío, la mía, los míos, las mías
el tuyo, la tuya, los tuyos, las tuyas
el suyo, la suya, los suyos, las suyas
el nuestro, la nuestra, los nuestros, las nuestras
el vuestro, la vuestra, los vuestros, las vuestras
el suyo, la suya, los suyos, las suyas

Yo tengo mi libro, no el tuyo.
Carmen tiene su cámara, no la tuya.
Aquí están tus billetes. ¿Dónde están los míos?
Aquí están tus maletas. ¿Dónde están las nuestras?

After the verb **ser** the definite article is normally omitted.

Aquellas maletas no son mías.

The definite article is used, however, for emphasis.

¿Aquella maleta? Es la mía, no la tuya.

Remember

Since the third person pronouns **el suyo**, etc., can mean so many things, they are often clarified by a prepositional phrase: **el de él, la de él, los de él, las de él, el de ella**, etc.

¿Tienes tu maleta?
Do you have your suitcase?

No, tengo la de ella.
No, I have hers.

14. Replace the italicized phrases with the appropriate possessive pronoun.

1. Tengo *mi cámara.*
2. *Tu cámara* saca mejores fotos que *mi cámara.*
3. Yo tengo *mis billetes* pero Carlos no sabe dónde están *sus billetes.*
4. Carlos busca *sus maletas* y *mis maletas.*
5. Hemos vendido *nuestra casa* pero no vamos a comprar *tu casa.*
6. ¿Dónde está *tu carro? Mi carro* está en el parqueo.
7. María prefiere *nuestro apartamento.*
8. ¿Tiene Ud. *su pasaporte* o *mi pasaporte?*
9. *Nuestros hijos* no están con *tus hijos* ahora.
10. Este paquete es *mi paquete,* el otro es *tu paquete.*
11. *Nuestra piscina* es más pequeña que *su piscina.*
12. Éstas son *mis revistas.* ¿Dónde están *tus revistas?*

Demonstrative Pronouns

The demonstrative pronouns are the same as the demonstrative adjectives, but they often carry a written accent mark to distinguish them from the adjective form.

éste	**ésta**	*this one (here)*
ése	**ésa**	*that one (there)*
aquél	**aquélla**	*that one (over there)*
éstos	**éstas**	*these (here)*
ésos	**ésas**	*those (there)*
aquéllos	**aquéllas**	*those (over there)*

Me gusta éste.
I like this one.

Pero prefiero ése (que tiene Ud.).
But I prefer that one (that you have).

Sin embargo, aquél es el mejor.
Nevertheless, that one (over there) is the best.

15. Complete the following sentences with the correct demonstrative pronoun.

    1. Esta novela es interesante pero prefiero _____ (que tiene Ud.).

    2. Aquellas casas son más pequeñas que _____ (aquí).

    3. Este carro cuesta menos que _____ (allá).

    4. La otra playa siempre tiene más gente que _____ (aquí).

Relative Pronouns

Que A relative pronoun introduces a clause that modifies a noun. The most commonly used relative pronoun in Spanish is **que**. It can replace either a person or a thing and can function as either the subject or the object of the clause.

> **La chica que canta es venezolana.**
> **El libro que está en la mesa es mi favorito.**
> **Los libros que escribe nuestro amigo son interesantes.**

The pronoun **que** can also be used after a preposition but only when it refers to a thing.

> **La novela de que hablas es de Azuela.**

A quien, A quienes The combination of the personal **a** (never translated into English) and the pronoun **quien** or **quienes** can replace the relative pronoun **que** when it indicates a person who is the direct object of the verb in the clause.

> **El señor que conocimos anoche es el presidente.**
> **El señor a quien conocimos anoche es el presidente.**

The pronoun **quien** must be used after a preposition when it refers to a person. **Que** after a preposition can refer only to things.

> **La chica en quien estoy pensando es venezolana, no cubana.**

El que, La que **El que, la que, los que,** and **las que** may also be used as the subject or object of a clause and replace either persons or things. They can replace **que** or **quien** when the speaker wishes to be extremely precise. They are equivalent to the English *the one who, the ones who.*

El que llega es mi hermano.
The one who is arriving is my brother.

Las que llegaron fueron mis hermanas.
The ones who arrived are (were) my sisters.

With Prepositions The pronouns **que** and **quien** are used after the short, common prepositions such as **de, con, por, para, a.** After longer prepositions, such as **alrededor de, tras, hacia, durante, cerca de, a través de, lejos de,** the long form **el que** of the relative pronoun is used.

The combinations **el cual, la cual, los cuales,** and **las cuales** can replace **el que,** etc., in certain constructions. They are not common in everyday conversational Spanish, however.

Lo que This is a neuter relative pronoun which is used to replace a general or abstract idea rather than a specific antecedent. It is similar to the English *what.*

Lo que necesitamos es más dinero.
What we need is more money.

No entiendo lo que está diciendo.
I don't understand what he is saying.

Cuyo The relative **cuyo** is equivalent to the English possessive *whose*. It agrees with the noun that it modifies, not with the possessor.

La señora cuyo hijo habla es directora de la escuela.
The woman whose son is speaking is the director of the school.

El señor cuyas maletas están aquí fue a sacar sus billetes.
The man whose suitcases are here went to buy his ticket.

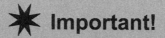 **Important!**

To ask the question *Whose (suitcases are they)?* you must say **¿De quién?**

¿De quién son las maletas?
Whose suitcases are they?

16. Complete the following sentences with the relative pronoun.

  1. El problema _____ discuten no es serio.
  2. La chica _____ acaba de entrar es mi hermana.
  3. Los libros _____ tú tienes son míos.
  4. El señor _____ conocimos anoche no está aquí.
  5. La botella _____ está en la mesa está vacía.
  6. Las chicas _____ invitamos son de la capital.

17. Rewrite the following sentences, substituting **que** with **a quien** or **a quienes**.

  1. El médico que llamamos vino en seguida.
  2. El señor que vimos acaba de llegar de Madrid.
  3. El niño que oímos estaba enfermo.
  4. Los amigos que espero no han llegado.
  5. La chica que vimos anoche es actriz.

18. Transform the following sentences according to the models.

Mi amigo llegó.
El que llegó fue mi amigo.

Mi amiga cantará.
La que cantará es mi amiga.

1. Don Pedro habló con el presidente.
2. La señora González salió primero.
3. Mis primos vinieron en avión.
4. Mi hermana bailará el fandango.
5. El dueño pagará los sueldos.

Chapter 5
PREPOSITIONS

✔ *Prepositions: Por and para*

Prepositions: *Por* and *Para*

The prepositions **por** and **para** have specific uses in Spanish. They are frequently translated as *for* but each has other uses and meanings.

The preposition **para** is used to indicate destination or purpose.

> **El barco salió para España.**
> *The ship left for Spain.*

> **Este regalo es para María.**
> *This gift is for Mary.*

> **Estudia para abogado.**
> *He is studying (to be) a lawyer.*

> **Lo quiero para mañana**.
> *I want it by tomorrow.*

The preposition **por** is used to indicate *through, along, by.*

> **Viajaron por España.**
> *They traveled through Spain.*

> **El barco pasó por las orillas.**
> *The ship passed by the shores.*

> **El ladrón entró por la ventana.**
> *The thief entered through the window.*

Por also has the meaning of *on behalf of, in favor of, instead of.*

> **Compré el regalo por María.**
> *I bought the gift for Mary.* (The gift is for another person, but Mary could not go to buy it so I went for her.)

> **Compré el regalo para María.**
> *I bought the gift for Mary.* (I am going to give the gift to Mary.)

The preposition **por** is used after the verbs **ir** *(to go),* **mandar** *(to send),* **volver** *(to return),* **venir** *(to come),* etc., in order to show the reason for an errand.

> **El niño fue por agua.**
> *The boy went for water.*

> **Vino por el médico.**
> *He came for the doctor.*

1. Complete the following sentences with **por** or **para.**
   1. El avión sale _____ San Juan.
   2. Ellos han pasado _____ aquí.
   3. Él va a la plaza _____ agua.
   4. Compré esta falda _____ Elena. Se la voy a dar mañana.
   5. Él entró _____ aquella puerta.
   6. ¿_____ quién es este libro?

7. Queremos viajar _____ Chile.
8. Ellos vendrán _____ ayuda.
9. El periódico es _____ papá.
10. Ella lo hará _____ María si ella no lo puede hacer.
11. Los turistas andaban _____ toda la ciudad.
12. Ellos salieron _____ las montañas.

Por is used to express a period of time.

> **Los árabes estuvieron en España por ocho siglos.**
> *The Arabs were in Spain for eight centuries.*

Por is also used to express an indefinite time or place.

> **Estarán aquí por diciembre.**
> *They will be here around December.*

> **Las llaves tienen que estar por aquí.**
> *The keys have to be around here.*

2. Complete the following sentences with **por** or **para**.
1. No estaré en la ciudad _____ dos meses.
2. Tienen que estar aquí _____ el día 25.
3. ¿_____ cuánto tiempo estarán Uds. aquí?
4. _____ primavera llegarán.
5. Tengo que hacerlo _____ mañana.
6. ¿Estará _____ aquí en la casa del señor González?

When **por** is followed by an infinitive, it expresses what remains to be done.

> **Queda mucho por hacer.**
> *There remains much to be done.*

When followed by an infinitive, **para** means *in order to*.

> **Necesito gafas para leer.**
> *I need glasses in order to read.*

The expression **estar por** means *to be inclined to, to be in the mood.*

> **Estoy por salir.**
> *I'm in the mood to leave.*

> **Están por divertirse.**
> *They're in the mood to have a good time.*

The expression **estar para** means *to be about to* or *to be ready to.*

> **Estamos para salir.**
> *We are ready to leave.*

> **Está para llover.**
> *It's about to rain*

3. Complete the following sentences with **por** or **para.**
   1. Quiero ir a mi alcoba _____ dormir.
   2. Queda la mitad de la novela _____ leer.
   3. Tiene que trabajar _____ ganarse la vida.
   4. El puente está _____ construir.

4. Complete the following sentences with **por** or **para.**
   1. Está _____ nevar.
   2. Él está _____ reñir (tener una disputa).
   3. Estamos listos _____ salir. Vámonos.
   4. Hace mucho tiempo que estoy aquí en casa. Estoy _____ salir.

Por is used to express manner, means, or motive.

> **Conducía a la niña por la mano.**
> *He was leading the little girl by the hand.*

> **La carta llegó por correo.**
> *The letter arrived by mail.*

> **Lucha por la libertad.**
> *He is fighting for freedom.*

Por is used to express *in exchange for.*

> **Él me dio cien dólares por el trabajo.**
> *He gave me a hundred dollars for the work.*

> **Cambié mi coche por otro.**
> *I exchanged my car for another one.*

Por is used to indicate measure, number, or rate.

> **Lo venden por docenas.**
> *They sell it by dozens.*

> **Vuela a quinientas millas por hora.**
> *It flies at 500 miles an hour.*

Por is used to express opinion or estimation.

> **Lo tomó por intelectual.**
> *He took him for an intellectual.*

> **Pasa por nativo.**
> *He passes for a native.*

Para is used to express a comparison of inequality (*Considering that he is . . . , In view of the fact that he is . . .*).

> **Para cubano, habla muy bien el inglés.**
> *He speaks English very well for a Cuban.*

5. Complete the following sentences with **por** or **para.**

1. Yo lo tomé _____ abogado pero es médico.
2. _____ extranjero, conoce muy bien nuestra ciudad.
3. Ellos luchan _____ su ideal.
4. Quiere vender la casa _____ cincuenta mil.
5. ¿Cuánto pagó Ud. _____ el cuadro?
6. Yo te doy este libro _____ el tuyo.
7. Él no lo hará _____ miedo de las consecuencias.
8. Yo lo voy a mandar _____ avión.
9. _____ niño, es muy inteligente.
10. Él lo vende _____ docenas.

Chapter 6
SPECIAL ISSUES

Ser and Estar

There are two verbs in Spanish both of which mean *to be* in English. Each has a particular range of meaning, and they are not interchangeable. The verb **ser** is derived from the Latin verb **esse** from which is also derived the English word "essence." The verb **ser** is therefore used to express an inherent quality or characteristic. The verb **estar**, on the other hand, is derived from the Latin verb **stare** from which is also derived the English word "state." The verb **estar** is therefore used to express a state or condition, often temporary.

With Predicate Nominative When a noun follows the verb *to be*, it is called the predicate nominative. Since in such a sentence the subject and predicate nominative are the same person or thing, the verb **ser** is always used.

> **El carbón es un mineral.**
> *Coal is a mineral.*

109

El señor González es abogado.
Mr. González is a lawyer.

Origin, Material, Ownership The verb **ser (de)** is used to tell where someone or something is from, what it is made of, to whom it belongs.

El señor González es de México.
Aquellos vinos son de Francia.
El anillo es de plata.
La casa es de madera.
Ese libro es de Juan.
El coche es del señor González.

Meaning "to take place" The verb **ser** is used to express "to take place" (**tener lugar**).

El concierto será mañana.
Será en el parque central.

Location The verb **estar** is used to express location. **Estar** is used to express both permanent and temporary location.

Carlos está ahora en Nueva York.
Madrid está en España.

Characteristic versus Condition When an adjective follows the verb *to be*, the use of the verb **ser** or **estar** depends upon the meaning conveyed. To express an inherent quality or characteristic, the verb **ser** is used.

La casa es moderna.
Carlos es guapo.
María es muy amable.

When the speaker wishes to imply that the subject belongs to a particular class or type, **ser** is used.

Estas frutas son agrias.
These fruits are sour. (They are the sour kind.)

In contrast to the verb **ser**, the verb **estar** is used when the speaker wishes to imply a temporary state or condition rather than an inherent characteristic.

> **El agua está fría.**
> **El café está caliente.**

Note the difference in the following sentences.

> **María es bonita.**
> *Mary is pretty. (She is a pretty person.)*
> **María está bonita hoy.**
> *Mary is pretty (today).*
> *(She is wearing something that*
> *makes her look pretty.)*

> **Estas frutas son agrias.**
> *These fruits are the sour kind.*
> **Estas frutas están agrias.**
> *These (particular) fruits are bitter.*
> *(Some of the same kind are sweet.)*

With words such as **soltero** *(bachelor)*, **casado** *(married)*, **viuda** *(widow)*, either **ser** or **estar** can be used. For example, to say **Estoy soltero** gives the meaning *I am (still) a bachelor.* To say **Soy soltero** gives the meaning *I am a bachelor* in the sense that I belong to the bachelor group.

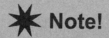 **Note!**

Note that the verb **estar** is used with **muerto** even though death is eternal. It is considered a state, in comparison to being alive.

> **Él está vivo.**
> **No está muerto.**

Changes of Meaning Certain words change meaning when used with **ser** or **estar**.

	With **ser**	With **estar**
aburrido	*boring*	*bored*
cansado	*tiresome*	*tired*
divertido	*amusing*	*amused*
enfermo	*sickly*	*sick*
listo	*clever*	*ready*
triste	*dull*	*sad*
vivo	*lively*	*alive*

Passive Voice The verb **ser** is used with a past participle to create the passive voice. **Estar** is used with a past participle to indicate the result of an action.

> **La puerta fue cerrada por el portero.**
> *The door was closed by the doorman.*

> **La puerta estaba cerrada.**
> *The door was closed.*

1. Complete the following sentences with the correct form of **ser** or **estar.**

   1. Madrid _____ la capital de España.
   2. La capital _____ en el centro del país.
   3. La fiesta _____ el ocho de julio en el restaurante Luna.
   4. El restaurante _____ en la calle San Martín.
   5. Las flores que _____ en la mesa _____ de nuestro jardín.
   6. El agua _____ muy fría hoy.
   7. Esta comida _____ riquísima. Tiene muy buen sabor.
   8. Y además la comida _____ muy buena para la salud.
   9. ¡Qué guapo _____ Carlos vestido de frac!
   10. Aquel señor _____ ciego.

11. Yo _____ ciego con tantas luces.
12. Todos estos productos _____ de Andalucía.
13. Aquel chico _____ de San Juan pero ahora
    _____ en Caracas.
14. La conferencia _____ aburrida y yo _____
    aburrido.
15. La corrida _____ en la Real Maestranza.
16. La plaza de toros _____ en las afueras de la
    ciudad.
17. La nieve _____ blanca.

2. Complete the following sentences with the correct form of **ser** or
estar.

1. Tienes que comer más verduras. Las verduras tienen muchas
   vitaminas y _____ muy buenas para la salud.
2. ¡Qué deliciosas! ¿Dónde compraste estas verduras?
   _____ muy buenas.
3. Él _____ tan aburrido que cada vez que empieza a
   hablar todo el mundo se duerme.
4. El pobre Carlos toma mucho. Siempre está bebiendo. No me
   gusta decirlo pero la verdad es que él _____
   borracho.
5. El pobre Tadeo _____ enfermo hoy. Anoche fue a
   una fiesta y tomó demasiado. Él _____ un poco
   borracho. Creo que hoy está sufriendo de una resaca.
6. No, no está enferma. Es su color. Ella _____ muy
   pálida.
7. No sé lo que le pasa a la pobre Marta. Tiene que estar
   enferma porque _____ muy pálida hoy.
8. No, no se murió el padre de Carlota. Él _____ vivo.
9. Él _____ muy vivo y divertido. A mí, como a todo el
   mundo, me gusta mucho estar con él.
10. El pobre Antonio _____ tan cansado que sólo quiere
    volver a casa para dormir un poquito.

Making a Sentence Negative

The most common way to make a sentence negative in Spanish is to place the word **no** before the verb.

Carlos conoce a María.	*Charles knows Mary.*
Carlos no conoce a María.	*Charles doesn't know Mary.*

If an object pronoun precedes the verb, the negative word **no** precedes the object pronoun.

Lo conozco.	*I know him.*
No lo conozco.	*I don't know him.*

Common Negative Words The most common negative words are:

nadie	*no one*
nada	*nothing*
nunca	*never*
ni... ni	*neither . . . nor*
ninguno	*no (used as an adjective)*

Study the following.

Affirmative	*Negative*
Alguien está aquí.	**Nadie está aquí.**
Veo a alguien.	**No veo a nadie.**
Tengo algo.	**No tengo nada.**
Algo está en la mesa.	**Nada está en la mesa.**
Él siempre va.	**Él nunca va. / Él no va nunca.**
¿Tienes un diccionario o una novela?	**¿No tienes ni diccionario ni novela?**
Tengo algún dinero.	**No tengo ningún dinero.**
Tiene alguna esperanza.	**No tiene ninguna esperanza.**

Note that the placement of the negative word in the sentence can vary. The negative word can precede the verb and be used alone or it can be used with **no** and follow the verb.

Nunca va.	**No va nunca.**

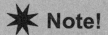

Note!

Unlike English, Spanish uses many negative words in the same sentence.

Carlos nunca dice nada a nadie.
Charles never says anything to anyone.

Tampoco *(not . . . either)* is the negative word that replaces **también** *(also)* in positive sentences.

Él lo sabe.	*He knows it.*
Yo lo sé también.	*I know it too.*

Él no lo sabe.	*He doesn't know it.*
Yo no lo sé tampoco.	*I don't know it either.*

Sino *(but)* is used after a negative sentence to contradict the negative statement. Its English meaning is *but rather*.

No quiero café, sino té.
I don't want coffee, but [rather] tea.

Special Negative Expressions Certain expressions have a negative meaning even though no negative word appears.

En mi vida, he oído tal cosa.
Never in my life have I heard such a thing.

En toda la noche, he podido dormir.
Not all night was I able to sleep. (I couldn't sleep at all last night.)

En el mundo se encontraría tal belleza.
Nowhere in the world would one find such beauty.

3. Rewrite the following sentences in the negative.

1. María tiene algo en la mano.
2. Algo está en la mesa.
3. Hay algo en la cocina.
4. Alguien estará a la puerta.
5. Allá veo a alguien.
6. ¿Tienes algún problema?
7. Él siempre dice la misma cosa.
8. Siempre vamos a las montañas.
9. ¿Tienes papel o lápiz?
10. Carlos siempre está hablando a alguien de algo.

4. Replace **también** with **tampoco** in the following sentences.

1. Él es rico también.
2. Ellos también tienen mucho dinero.
3. María lo sabe y yo lo sé también.
4. También viene Juan.

5. Follow the model.

> **feo / guapo**
> **Él no es feo, sino guapo.**

1. estúpido / inteligente
2. bajo / alto
3. gordo / flaco
4. pobre / rico
5. perezoso / ambicioso

Special Uses of Certain Verbs

Acabar The verb acabar means *to finish* and is synonymous with the verb **terminar.**

> **Ellos acabaron (terminaron) ayer.**
> *They finished yesterday.*

The expression **acabar de** means *to have just (done something)*. This expression is used in two tenses only: the present and the imperfect.

Acaban de llegar.
They have just arrived.

Acababan de llegar cuando salimos.
They had just arrived when we left.

The expression **acabar por** means *to end up*.

Yo acabé por creerlo.
I ended up believing it.

Acordarse de, Recordar These verbs mean *to remember*, and they can be used interchangeably.

No recuerdo nada.
I don't remember anything.

No me acuerdo de nada.
I don't remember anything.

Andar, Ir, Irse The verb **andar** means *to go* as does the verb **ir**. Andar applies to the motion of inanimate objects and animals. It can also be used with people when no idea of destination is expressed in the sentence.

El perro anda por aquí.
The dog is (going) around here [somewhere].

¿Qué ha pasado? Mi reloj no anda.
What happened? My watch isn't running.

Aquel señor anda sin zapatos.
That man is going [around]without shoes.

Los turistas andan por el parque.
The tourists are wandering through the park.

Ir means to go to a particular destination, in a specific direction or for a definite purpose.

> **Vamos a España.**
> *We are going to Spain.*

> **Tienes que ir a la izquierda.**
> *You have to go left.*

> **Ellos van por ayuda.**
> *They are going for help.*

Irse means *to go away, to leave.* It is usually used alone but you will sometimes hear it used with a destination with the preposition **para** or **a**.

> **Nos vamos ahora.**
> *We are leaving now.*

> **Me voy. Adiós.**
> *I'm leaving. Good-bye!*

> **Ya se van para Extremadura.**
> *They are going off to Extremadura.*

Two useful expressions are: **¡Vámonos!** which means *Let's go!* and **¡Ya voy!** which means *I'm coming.*

Cuidar, Cuidarse The verb **cuidar** can be followed by either the preposition **a** or **de**, and it means *to care for* or *to take care of.*

> **Él cuida de (a) los niños.**
> *He is taking care of the children.*

The reflexive form **cuidarse** means *to take care of oneself.*

> **Él se cuida bien.**
> *He takes (good) care of himself.*

Cuidarse de means *to care about.*

> **Él no se cuida de mi opinión. No le importa nada.**
> *He does not care about my opinion. It means nothing to him.*

Dar The verb **dar** *to give* is used in many expressions. **Dar un paseo** means *to take a walk.*

> **Vamos a dar un paseo por el parque.**
> *Let's take a walk through the park.*

Dar a means *to face.*

> **Ella tiene un cuarto que da al mar.**
> *She has a room that faces the sea.*

The expression **dar a entender** means *to give (lead) one to understand.*

> **Él me dio a entender que él aceptaría el puesto.**
> *He led me to understand that he would accept the job.*

Dar con means *to run into (someone)* unexpectedly.

> **Di con mi mejor amigo en la calle.**
> *I ran into my my best friend on the street.*

Dar de is used in expressions such as *to give (someone) something to drink* or *to eat.*

> **Ella dio de beber al niño.**
> *She gave the child something to drink.*

> **Tengo que dar de comer al perro.**
> *I have to give the dog something to eat.*

Dar por means *to consider as, to believe to be, to take for,* etc.

> **Ellos me dieron por muerto.**
> *They thought that I was dead.* (or *They gave me up for dead.*)

> The verb **dar** is also used in the expression **dar las** (**horas**), which means *to strike* when referring to time.
>
> **Dieron las cuatro.** *It struck four.*

¿Qué más da? means *What difference does it make?* **Me da lo mismo** or **Me da igual** means *It's all the same to me.*

Dejar This verb means *to leave* in the sense of *to leave (something) behind.*

    ¡Ay, Dios! Dejé el paquete en el autobús.
    Oh, Gosh! I left the package on the bus.

The expression **dejar de** means *to fail* or *to stop.*

    Él dejó de hacerlo.   *He failed to do it.*
    Él dejó de fumar.   *He stopped smoking.*

Hacer The verb **hacer** is used in weather expressions.

    Hace buen tiempo.
    The weather is good.

    Hace frío en el invierno.
    It's cold in winter.

    Pero ahora está haciendo mucho calor.
    But now it's very hot.

Hacerse, Llegar a ser, Ponerse, Volverse These verbs all mean *to become*. Each one, however, has a slightly different usage. **Hacerse** means to become something after making a certain effort.

> **Roberto se hizo abogado.**
> *Robert became a lawyer.*

Llegar a ser means to become something after expending a great deal of effort.

> **Llegó a ser presidente de la compañía.**
> *He became (finally got to be) president of the company.*

Ponerse means to become something involuntarily, not purposely.

> **Ella se puso roja.**   *She turned red.*
> **Él se puso gordo.**   *He got fat.*

Volverse means to become something which is completely unexpected or a complete reversal.

> **El pobre señor se volvió loco.**
> *The poor man went crazy.*

> **Se volvieron republicanos.**
> *They became Republicans.*

Jugar, Tocar The verb **jugar** means *to play a game or a sport,* or *to gamble*. It may be followed by the preposition **a** with sports. The preposition **a** is always used in Spain but is omitted in many areas of Latin America.

> **Ella juega muy bien (al) fútbol.**
> *She plays football well.*

> **Los niños están jugando en el jardín.**
> *The children are playing in the garden.*

Él juega mucho y siempre pierde.
He gambles a lot and always loses.

The verb **tocar** means *to play* a musical instrument.

Ella toca el piano.   *She plays the piano.*

Pensar en, Pensar de Both verbs mean *to think about*. **Pensar en** also means *to ponder* or *consider*. **Pensar de** refers to an opinion.

Él está pensando en el asunto.
He's thinking about the situation.

¿Qué piensas del asunto?
What do you think about the situation?

Poner The verb **poner** literally means *to put* or *to place*. It can also mean *to turn on*.

Quiero poner la radio.
I want to turn on the radio.

Ponerse means *to put on* (*clothing*).

Él se puso la chaqueta.
He put on his jacket.

Ponerse a means *to begin* or *to start*.

Ellos se pusieron a reír.
They started laughing.

Quedar The verb **quedar** means *to remain* or *to stay*.

¿Cuánto tiempo quedaron ellos en España?
How long did they stay in Spain?

Quedar can also mean *to be* in the sense of *to be located.*

¿Dónde queda la biblioteca?
Where is the library?

Quedar can also mean *to be left.*

Ahora me quedan sólo dos.
Now I have only two left.

Quedarse can mean *to stay* in the sense of *to keep* or *to lodge.*

Vamos a salir de la carretera. Quédese en el carril derecho.
We're going to get off the highway. Stay in the right lane.

Quédese con las llaves.
Keep the keys.

Nos quedamos en aquel hotel.
We stayed in that hotel.

Quedar en means *to agree on* something.

Ellos han quedado en reunirse de nuevo mañana.
They have agreed to meet again tomorrow.

Saber, Conocer Both of these verbs mean *to know.* **Saber** means to know a fact, a reason, a subject, to know how to. Its object is knowledge that can be passed on to another person.

Él sabe los resultados.
He knows the results.

Él sabe matemáticas.
He knows math.

¿Sabes tocar la guitarra?
Do you know how to play the guitar?

Conocer involves personal familiarity (with a person, a country, literature).

> **Conozco a Juan.**
> *I know John.*

> **Conocemos la literatura española.**
> *We are acquainted with Spanish literature.*

The expression **saber a** means *to taste like (have the flavor of)*.

> **No me gusta. Sabe a vinagre.**
> *I don't like it. It tastes like vinegar.*

Servir para, *Servir de* These verbs mean *to be of use as* or *to serve as*.

> **Esto sirve para abrir botellas.**
> *This is used to open bottles.*

> **La verdad es que esto no sirve para nada.**
> *The truth is that this is of no use whatever.*

> **Él nos sirve de guía.**
> *He is serving as our guide.*

Servirse de means *to make use of*.

> **Él se sirve de eso para abrir botellas.**
> *He uses this to open bottles.*

The expression **sírvase** is a polite way of saying *please*.

> **Sírvase usar este plato**.
> *Please use this plate.*

Tener The verb **tener** is used with nouns such as hunger, thirst, etc., for which English uses the verb *to be*.

| **Tengo hambre.** | *I'm hungry.* |
| **Tengo sed.** | *I'm thirsty.* |

Tener que means *to have to*.

Tengo que salir ahora.
I have to leave now.

Tener que ver means *to have to do with* someone or something.

Eso no tiene nada que ver con el proyecto (conmigo).
This has nothing to do with the project (with me).

¿Qué tiene? means *What's the matter?*

¿Qué tiene él? Me parece que está muy nervioso.
What's the matter with him? He seems to me to be very nervous.

Aquí tiene means *Here is* when handing someone something.

Aquí tiene Ud. el libro que me pidió.
Here is the book you asked me for.

Volver, Devolver, Envolver The verb **volver** means *to return* from somewhere.

Yo vuelvo de Madrid.
I am returning from Madrid.

Ellos vuelven a las ocho.
They are returning at eight.

The verb **devolver** *to return* in the sense *to give back*.

Él me devolvió el dinero que me debía.
He returned the money that he owed me.

The verb **envolver** means *to wrap*.

> **Envolvieron el paquete.**
> *They wrapped the package.*

Volver a means *to do again* or *to repeat* the action of the infinitive.

> **Él volvió a leer el libro.**
> *He read the book again.*

Volver en sí means *to come to*.

> **Él se desmayó pero volvió en sí en la ambulancia.**
> *He fainted, but he came to in the ambulance.*

Answers

Chapter 1

1.
1. el
2. la, la
3. las, la
4. el, el, la
5. el, el
6. la
7. los
8. el
9. las, el, la
10. los
11. la, la, la
12. el
13. el
14. el, los, el
15. la
16. la, los

2.
1. Las cantidades son enormes.
2. Los dramas son muy buenos.
3. Las ciudades son bonitas.
4. Las fotos son bonitas.
5. Los coches son modernos.
6. Las casas son bonitas.
7. Los edificios son altos.
8. Los presidentes son viejos.
9. Las amistades son importantes.
10. Las civilizaciones son antiguas.

3.
1. los
2. el, un
3. el, un
4. la
5. el
6. *nothing*
7. *nothing*
8. el, un
9. los
10. el, *nothing, nothing*
11. la, *nothing*
12. las
13. el, un
14. las

Chapter 2

1.
1. bonita, moderna
2. grande, muchas
3. blancas
4. antiguo, tropicales
5. estupenda
6. fáciles, difíciles
7. aquel, lujoso, deliciosas
8. aquellos, alemanes
9. cubanas, españolas, sabrosas
10. aquellos, delgados, enfermos
11. fuertes
12. mis
13. estrechas, este, pintorescas
14. buen
15. esta, interesante, cien
16. gran, español
17. bonitas, oriental
18. amargo, dulce
19. inteligentes, buenas
20. mejores
21. hablador, holgazana
22. nuestros, españoles
23. azul claro, café
24. rosa
25. marrón (marrones), beige

2.
1. Estas novelas son mejores que las otras.
2. Los señores argentinos hablan de los grandes autores.
3. Estas señoras altas son inglesas.
4. Aquellos montes están cubiertos de nieve.
5. Estos chicos son más altos y fuertes que aquellos chicos.

127

6. Estas niñas son las menores de la familia.
7. Estos artículos son tan interesantes como los otros.
8. Los campos verdes están en las regiones occidentales.

3. 1. Juan es más alto que Roberto.
2. Changhai es la ciudad más grande del mundo.
3. Elena tiene tanto dinero como Roberto.
4. Teresa es la más inteligente de la clase.
5. El Misisipí es el río más largo de los Estados Unidos.
6. Tulúa tiene tantos habitantes como Riobomba.
7. Aquellos señores tienen la finca.
8. Juan tiene tus (sus) libros.
9. Sus fotografías están en la maleta.
10. Teresa es tan bonita como Elena.

CHAPTER 3
1. 1. conozco
2. sirven
3. vivimos
4. hablamos
5. come
6. salgo
7. hacen
8. prefiere
9. pedimos
10. construyen
11. vuelves
12. podemos
13. oigo
14. dice, cuesta
15. sabemos, juega
16. pongo, mando
17. vengo, vas
18. sé, dice
19. vivimos
20. nadan
21. digo, sé, conozco
22. pueden, quieren
23. repito, soy
24. dice, sabe, están

2. 1. estamos
2. llega
3. sale
4. muero
3. estaba, era, era, quedaba, tenía, era, tenía, estaba, trabajaba, encontraba, tenía, quería, podía, tenía, necesitaba, ganaba, mandaba, eran, estaba, podía, tenía, hacía, nevaba, tenía, alquilaba, tenía

4. 1. hicieron
2. tradujiste
3. quiso
4. pusieron
5. estuvo
6. trajo
7. cantaron, tocó
8. vinimos
9. pudiste
10. dijo
11. supe
12. comió
13. oyeron
14. pidió
15. tuvimos

5. 1. La compañía no tuvo suficientes fondos económicos.
2. ¿Por qué viniste a las ocho de la mañana?
3. Él no pudo ayudarme.
4. Tú buscaste los informes.
5. Nosotros anduvimos por la capital.
6. ¿Quién te lo dijo?

7. Los alumnos no lo supieron.
8. Yo fui en tren.
9. Ellos no estuvieron aquí.
10. ¿Por qué no lo pusimos en el garage?
11. Él no leyó el programa del día.
12. No lo hicimos sin ayuda.

6. 1. Ellos miraban la televisión cada noche.
2. Juan estuvo aquí el otro día también.
3. Íbamos allá muy a menudo.
4. Comieron en aquel restaurante el sábado pasado.
5. Yo lo veía con frecuencia.
6. Siempre discutíamos el mismo problema.
7. El profesor lo repitió una vez.
8. El director desaparecía de vez en cuando.
9. Su padre estuvo enfermo por tres años.
10. Durante todos sus viajes, él pagaba con cheques de viajero.

7. 1. nadaban, tomaban
2. hablaba, entré
3. discutían, interrumpimos
4. preparaba, ponía
5. dormía, sonó
6. comían, llamé
7. miraban, estudiaba
8. hablaban, anuncié
9. llegaron, hacía
10. bailaban, cantaban

8. 1. discutirá
2. hablaré
3. estarás
4. comeremos
5. recibirán
6. volveremos
7. contaré

8. comprará
9. venderemos
10. llegará

9. 1. Ellos harán un viaje.
2. Carlitos no querrá salir.
3. Yo tendré bastante tiempo.
4. ¿Cuánto valdrá la joya?
5. Nosotros saldremos a las ocho en punto.
6. Tú dirás la verdad.
7. Uds. vendrán en avión, ¿no?
8. Yo sabré los resultados.
9. ¿Por qué no podrás jugar?
10. Todos no cabrán en el mismo carro.

10. 1. nadarían
2. escribiría
3. pagaría
4. venderíamos
5. vivirían

11. 1. haría
2. tendrías
3. tendría, sería
4. haría
5. tendría
6. tendría
7. podríamos
8. devolvería
9. querría
10. daría

12. 1. han estado
2. ha cantado
3. ha contestado
4. han empezado
5. he hablado
6. has comido

13. 1. habíamos llegado
2. habían comido
3. habías preparado

4. había conocido
5. había vuelto
6. había roto
7. había dicho
8. habíamos hecho

14. 1. Yo habría terminado pero no tenía tiempo.
2. Él habría bebido algo pero no tenía sed.
3. Ellos habrían dormido pero no tenían sueño.
4. Nosotros nos habríamos puesto una chaqueta pero no teníamos frío.
5. Yo me habría quitado el suéter pero no tenía calor.
6. Tú habrías hecho algo pero tenías miedo.

15. 1. hablen, coman, escriban, vuelvan, duerman, sigan, vengan, salgan, conduzcan
2. terminemos, prometamos, empecemos, sirvamos, volvamos, salgamos, estemos presentes, vayamos
3. trabaje, lea, insista, siga, venga, duerma, salga, conduzca, vaya, sea así
4. estudies, comas, vuelvas, salgas, duermas

16. 1. Es importante que nosotros recibamos los resultados.
2. Conviene que ellos lleguen por la mañana.
3. Es necesario que el chico estudie más.
4. Es posible que ellos vuelvan pronto.
5. Es imposible que el héroe pierda el juego.
6. Es mejor que todos estén presentes.

17. 1. estarán   5. asista
2. puedas   6. hagan
3. tengan   7. contestará
4. volveremos   8. lleguen

18. 1. trabaje, estudie, coma, lea, escriba
2. compren, vendan, pidan, sirvan, hagan, traigan, traduzcan
3. fume, salga, vaya, siga, duerma
4. esperemos, trabajemos, prometamos, volvamos, salgamos, conduzcamos

19. 1. habla español, escribe bien, conoce la computadora
2. hable español, escriba bien, conozca la computadora

20. 1. terminara
2. bebiéramos
3. cantáramos
4. vivieras
5. estudiara
6. saliera
7. tradujéramos
8. volvieran
9. fueran
10. hablaras

21. 1. Insistían en que comiéramos con ellos.
2. Tenían miedo de que no volvieras.
3. Ella prefería que vinieras a las ocho.
4. Querían que hiciéramos el viaje en tren.
5. Insistía en que tú lo repitieras.
6. Temían que no lo supiéramos.

22. 1. hablemos, comencemos, comamos, salgamos, lleguemos, sirvamos

2. hablamos, comenzamos, comimos, salimos, llegamos, servimos
3. terminen, canten, coman, salgan, lleguen, vuelvan
4. terminaron, cantaron, comieron, salieron, llegaron, volvieron
5. hable, termine, vuelva, salga
6. hablara, entrara, terminara, volviera, saliera

23. 1. esté
2. llueve
3. trabaje
4. sea

24. 1. ayuden   4. fueran
2. ayudaras   5. vayan
3. lleguen

25. 1. hayas llegado
2. hayamos dicho
3. hayan conocido
4. haya terminado
5. hayan sufrido
6. haya pasado

26. 1. hubiera comido
2. hubieran sabido
3. hubiéramos discutido
4. hubieran salido
5. hubieras terminado

27. 1. tienen
2. llueve
3. acompañas
4. estuviera
5. pudiéramos
6. tuvieras
7. hubiera sabido
8. hubiera salido

28. 1. tome   7. pague
2. siga   8. siga

3. doble   9. salga
4. vaya   10. vire
5. tome   11. siga
6. siga   12. tenga

29. 1. Sí, nada.   5. Sí, lee.
2. Sí, canta.   6. Sí, come.
3. Sí, baila.   7. Sí, escribe
4. Sí, trabaja.   la carta.

30. 1. Ten suerte.
2. Ten tiempo.
3. Pon todo en orden.
4. Pon la mesa.
5. Ven en seguida.
6. Ven mañana.
7. Sal ahora.
8. Sal de noche.

31. 1. No hables.
2. No nades.
3. No comas.
4. No bebas.
5. No escribas.
6. No pienses.
7. No vuelvas.
8. No pidas.
9. No sirvas.
10. No vengas.
11. No salgas más.
12. No tengas más paciencia.

32. 1. María está cantando y Juan está tocando la guitarra.
2. Las chicas están preparando la lección.
3. Yo estoy poniendo la mesa.
4. Estamos comiendo en el restaurante.
5. El avión está saliendo.
6. Ellos están viviendo con nosotros.

33. 1. Él estaba charlando con sus amigos.

2. Ellos estaban haciendo un viaje por España.
3. Aquellos señores estaban trabajando como bestias.
4. Yo no estaba comiendo nada.
5. Él estaba saliendo con María.
6. El profesor estaba explicando la teoría.
7. Estábamos construyendo una carretera en el interior.
8. Ella no estaba pidiendo nada.

34.
1. me
2. se
3. se
4. nos
5. te
6. se

35.
1. me acuesto
2. se baña
3. nos cepillamos
4. se mira, se peina
5. te sientas

36.
1. la
2. la
3. mi
4. el
5. tu
6. los

37.
1. se
2. *nothing*
3. *nothing*
4. se
5. *nothing*
6. nos
7. me
8. me, *nothing*

38.
1. fue, por
2. fue, por
3. fue, por
4. fueron, por

39.
1. se cierra
2. se dice
3. se usa
4. se ven
5. se hacen
6. se abre

CHAPTER 4

1.
1. nosotros
2. tú
3. nosotros
4. yo
5. tú
6. Ud.
7. yo

2.
1. yo
2. nosotros
3. tú (Ud.)
4. él

3.
1. la
2. las
3. lo
4. lo
5. la
6. los

4. te, me, te, me, te

5.
1. Él le dijo la verdad (a ella).
2. El cartero le dio las cartas (a él).
3. El señor González les habló (a ellos).
4. Yo le di un regalo (a ella).

6.
1. Mamá me los compró.
2. Mamá me la compró.
3. Mamá me las compró.
4. Mamá me los compró.

7.
1. Carlos se las dio (a ella).
2. Yo se lo mandé (a él).
3. El profesor se la explicó (a ellos).
4. La madre se lo compró (a ella).
5. El pasajero se los dio (a él).
6. María se lo leyó (a ellas).

8.
1. Ella te lo quiere dar.
Ella quiere dártelo.
2. Se lo queremos devolver (a él).
Queremos devolvérselo (a él).
3. Se la van a servir (a él).
Van a servírsela (a él).
4. El presidente la prefiere dar.
El presidente prefiere darla.
5. Ellos lo piensan vender.
Ellos piensan venderlo.

9.
1. Te la están cantando.
Están cantándotela.
2. Se lo está dedicando (a él).
Están dedicándoselo (a él).

3. Se la estamos sirviendo (a ellos).
   Estamos sirviéndosela (a ellos).
4. Ella me las está mostrando.
   Ella está mostrándomelas.
5. Él te lo está preparando.
   Él está preparándotelo.

10. 1. Súbalas Ud.
2. Dígamelo Ud.
3. Pídala Ud.
4. Lávenlos Uds.
5. Búscalo.
6. Prepáramela.
7. Véndelos.
8. No lo lea Ud.
9. No los sirvan Uds.
10. No la saque Ud.
11. No la pongas en la mesa.
12. No se lo dé Ud. (a él).

11. 1. Sí, levantémonos.
   No, no nos levantemos.
2. Sí, lavémonos la cara.
   No, no nos lavemos la cara.
3. Sí, preparémonos.
   No, no nos preparemos.
4. Sí, quitémonos la corbata.
   No, no nos quitemos la corbata.

12. 1. me, -e
2. me, -en
3. nos, -a
4. nos, -an
5. te, -an

13. 1. Nos gusta la música.
2. Le gustan las lenguas.
3. Les gusta el proyecto.
4. Te gustan los programas.
5. A Elena le gusta el arte moderno.

14. 1. Tengo la mía.
2. La tuya saca mejores fotos que la mía.
3. Yo tengo los míos pero Carlos no sabe dónde están los suyos.
4. Carlos busca las suyas y las mías.
5. Hemos vendido la nuestra pero no vamos a comprar la tuya.
6. ¿Dónde está el tuyo? El mío está en el parqueo.
7. María prefiere el nuestro.
8. ¿Tiene Ud. el suyo o el mío?
9. Los nuestros no están con los tuyos ahora.
10. Este paquete es (el) mío, el otro es (el) tuyo.
11. La nuestra es más pequeña que la suya.
12. Éstas son (las) mías. ¿Dónde están las tuyas?

15. 1. ésa   3. aquél
2. éstas   4. ésta

16. *All answers are* que.

17. 1. El médico a quien llamamos vino en seguida.
2. El señor a quien vimos acaba de llegar de Madrid.
3. El niño a quien oímos estaba enfermo.
4. Los amigos a quienes espero no han llegado.
5. La chica a quien vimos anoche es actriz.

18. 1. El que habló con el presidente fue don Pedro.
2. La que salió primero fue la señora González.

3. Los que viniveron en avión fueron mis primos.
4. La que bailará el fandango es mi prima.
5. El que pagará los sueldos es el dueño.

CHAPTER 5
1. 1. para 7. por
2. por 8. por
3. por 9. para
4. para 10. por
5. por 11. por
6. para 12. para

2. 1. por 4. por
2. para 5. para
3. por 6. por

3. 1. para 3. para
2. por 4. por

4. 1. para
2. para *(if he is getting ready to);* por *(if he is annoyed and wants to)*
3. para
4. por

5. 1. por 6. por
2. para 7. por
3. por 8. por
4. por 9. para
5. por 10. por

CHAPTER 6
1. 1. es 10. es
2. está 11. estoy
3. es 12. son
4. está 13. es, está

5. están, son 14. es, estoy
6. está 15. es
7. está 16. está
8. es 17. es
9. está

2. 1. son 6. es
2. están 7. está
3. es 8. está
4. es 9. es
5. está, estaba 10. cstá

3. 1. María no tiene nada en la mano.
2. Nada está en la mesa.
3. No hay nada en la cocina.
4. Nadie estará a la puerta.
5. Allá no veo a nadie.
6. ¿No tienes ningún problema?
7. Él nunca dice la misma cosa.
8. Nunca vamos a las montañas.
9. ¿No tienes ni papel ni lápiz?
10. Carlos nunca está hablando a nadie de nada.

4. 1. Él no es rico tampoco.
2. Ellos tampoco tienen mucho dinero.
3. María no lo sabe y yo no lo sé tampoco.
4. Tampoco viene Juan.

5. 1. Él no es estupído, sino inteligente.
2. Él no es bajo, sino alto.
3. Él no es gordo, sino flaco.
4. Él no es pobre, sino rico.
5. Él no es perezoso, sino ambicioso.

Index